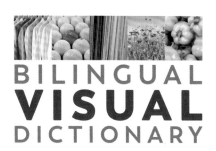

BILINGUAL
VISUAL
DICTIONARY

BILINGUAL VISUAL DICTIONARY

FIRST EDITION

Senior Editors Angeles Gavira, Angela Wilkes
Senior Art Editor Ina Stradins
Designed for DK by WaltonCreative.com
Language content for DK by g-and-w publishing

REVISED EDITION

DK LONDON

Senior Editor Christine Stroyan
Project Editor Sophie Adam
Designer Thomas Keenes
Managing Editor Carine Tracanelli
Managing Art Editor Anna Hall
Senior Production Controller Poppy David, Meskerem Berhane
Senior Jacket Designer Surabhi Wadhwa Gandhi
Jacket Design Development Manager Sophia MTT
Translations by Andiamo! Language Services Ltd
Art Editor Karen Self
Associate Publishing Director Liz Wheeler
Publishing Director Jonathan Metcalf

DK INDIA

Editor Alka Thakur-Hazarika
Desk Editors Pankhoori Sinha, Joicy John
DTP Designers Anurag Trivedi, Rakesh Sharma
Assistant Picture Researchers Geetam Biswas, Shubhdeep Kaur
Senior Art Editor Vikas Chauhan
Managing Editor Saloni Singh
Managing Art Editor Govind Mittal
DTP Coordinator Tarun Sharma
Preproduction Manager Balwant Singh
Senior Jacket Coordinator Priyanka Sharma Saddi

DK US

US Proofreader Heather Wilcox
US Executive Editor Lori Cates Hand

This American Edition, 2024
First American Edition, 2005
Published in the United States by DK Publishing,
a division of Penguin Random House LLC
1745 Broadway, 20th Floor, New York, NY 10019

contenido
contents

42
la salud
health

146
comer fuera
eating out

252
el ocio
leisure

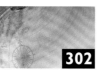

español • english

comer fuera
eating out

el estudio • study

el trabajo • work

el transporte
transportation

los deportes • sports

el ocio • leisure

el medio ambiente
environment

los datos
reference

sobre el diccionario

Está comprobado que el empleo de fotografías ayuda a la comprensión y a la retención de información. Basados en este principio, este diccionario bilingüe y altamente ilustrado exhibe un amplio registro de vocabulario útil y actual en dos idiomas europeos.

El diccionario aparece dividido según su temática y abarca la mayoría de los aspectos del mundo cotidiano con detalle.

Este diccionario es un instrumento de referencia esencial para todo aquél que esté interesado en los idiomas; es práctico, estimulante y fácil de usar.

Algunos puntos a observar

Los dos idiomas se presentan siempre en el mismo orden: español (mejicano y castellano) e inglés. Cuando existen diferencias entre el castellano y el español mejicano, el mejicano aparece primero seguido por el castellano; este último entre paréntesis e indicado con una ^C: **la llave** (^C**el grifo**).

En español, los sustantivos son masculinos o femeninos, y el artículo definido es "el" o "la" respectivamente ("los" o "las" para el plural):

el menú	**los cacahuates**
menu	peanuts
la semilla	**las almendras**
seed	almonds

Los adjetivos y las palabras para personas y profesiones se indican con una *m* para la forma masculina y con una *f* para la forma femenina.

el abogado *m*	**fresco** *m*
la abogada *f*	**fresca** *f*
lawyer	fresh

Los verbos se indican con una (v) después del inglés:

cosechar | harvest (v)

Cada idioma tiene su propio índice. Aquí podrá mirar una palabra en cualquiera de los dos idiomas y se le indicará el número de la página donde aparece. El género se indica con una *m* o una *f*.

cómo utilizar este libro

Ya se encuentre aprendiendo un idioma nuevo por motivos de trabajo, placer, o para preparar sus vacaciones al extranjero, o ya quiera ampliar su vocabulario en un idioma que ya conoce, este diccionario es un instrumento muy valioso que podrá utilizar de distintas maneras.

Cuando esté aprendiendo un idioma nuevo, busque palabras similares en distintos idiomas y palabras que parecen similares pero que poseen significados totalmente distintos. También podrá observar cómo los idiomas se influyen unos a otros. Por ejemplo, la lengua inglesa ha importado muchos términos de comida de otras lenguas pero, a cambio, ha exportado términos empleados en tecnología y cultura popular.

Actividades prácticas de aprendizaje

• Mientras se desplaza por su casa, lugar de trabajo o colegio, intente mirar las páginas que se refieren a ese lugar. Podrá entonces cerrar el libro, mirar a su alrededor y ver cuántos objetos o características puede nombrar.

• Desafíese a usted mismo a escribir una historia, carta o diálogo empleando tantos términos de una página concreta como le sea posible. Esto le ayudará a retener vocabulario y recordar la ortografía. Si quiere ir progresando para poder escribir un texto más largo, comience con frases que incorporen 2 ó 3 palabras.

• Si tiene buena memoria visual, intente dibujar o calcar objetos del libro; luego cierre el libro y escriba las palabras correspondientes debajo del dibujo.

• Cuando se sienta más seguro, escoja palabras del índice de uno de los idiomas y vea si sabe lo que significan antes de consultar la página correspondiente para comprobarlo.

app de audio gratuita

Esta app de audio incluye todas las palabras y frases del libro, leídas por hablantes nativos tanto de español como de inglés, para facilitar el aprendizaje de vocabulario importante y mejorar la pronunciación. También hay una versión de audio disponible para el resto de los libros de la serie.

cómo utilizar la app de audio

• Busque "DK Visual Dictionary" en la tienda de aplicaciones de su elección y descárguela de forma gratuita en tu teléfono o tableta.

• Abre la app y elige la edición de su libro.

• Seleccione tu libro en el menú "Choose your book" (elige tu libro).

• Seleccione un capítulo del índice de contenidos o introduzca el número de página en la barra de búsqueda.

• Ordene las palabras de la A a la Z en español o inglés.

• Desplácese hacia arriba o hacia abajo por la lista para encontrar una palabra o frase.

• Para escuchar una palabra, pulsa sobre ella.

about the dictionary

The use of pictures is proven to aid understanding and the retention of information. Working on this principle, this highly illustrated bilingual dictionary presents a large range of useful current vocabulary in two European languages.

The dictionary is divided thematically and covers most aspects of the everyday world in detail.

This is an essential reference tool for anyone interested in languages—practical, stimulating, and easy-to-use.

A few things to note

The two languages are always presented in the same order—Spanish and English. Where a word or phrase is different in Castilian and Mexican Spanish, the Mexican appears first, followed by the Castilian; the latter in brackets and indicated by a ^C: la **llave** (^C**el grifo**).

In Spanish, nouns are masculine or feminine, and the definite article is "el" or "la" respectively ("los" or "las" for plurals).

el menú	**los cacahuates**
menu	peanuts

la semilla	**las almendras**
seed	almonds

Adjectives and words for people and professions are indicated with *m* for masculine and *f* for feminine.

el abogado *m*	**fresco** *m*
la abogada *f*	**fresca** *f*
lawyer	fresh

Verbs are indicated by a (v) after the English, for example:

cosechar | harvest (v)

Each language also has its own index at the back of the book. Here you can look up a word in either of the two languages and be referred to the page number(s) where it appears. The gender is indicated with *m* or *f*.

how to use this book

Whether you are learning a new language for business, pleasure, or in preparation for a holiday abroad, or are hoping to extend your vocabulary in an already familiar language, this dictionary is a valuable learning tool which you can use in a number of different ways.

When learning a new language, look out for cognates (words that are alike in different languages) and false friends (words that look alike but carry significantly different meanings). You can also see where the languages have influenced each other. For example, English has imported many terms for food from other European languages but, in turn, exported terms used in technology and popular culture.

Practical learning activities

• As you move about your home, workplace, or college, try looking at the pages which cover that setting. You could then close the book, look around you and see how many of the objects and features you can name.
• Challenge yourself to write a story, letter, or dialogue using as many of the terms on a particular page as possible. This will help you retain the vocabulary and remember the spelling. If you want to build up to writing a longer text, start with sentences incorporating 2–3 words.
• If you have a very visual memory, try drawing or tracing items from the book onto a piece of paper, then close the book and fill in the words below the picture.
• Once you are more confident, pick out words in a foreign-language index and see if you know what they mean before turning to the relevant page to check if you were right.

free audio app

The DK Visual Dictionary app contains all the words and phrases in the book, spoken by native speakers in both Spanish and English, making it easier to learn important vocabulary and improve your pronunciation. Audio is also available for all the other books in the series.

how to use the audio app

• Search for "DK Visual Dictionary" in your chosen app store and download the free app on your smartphone or tablet.
• Open the app and select your edition of the book.
• Select your book from the "Choose your book" menu.
• Select a chapter from the contents list or enter a page number in the search bar.
• Sort the words A–Z in Spanish or English.
• Scroll up or down through the list to find a word or phrase.
• Tap a word to hear it.

la gente
people

el cuerpo • body

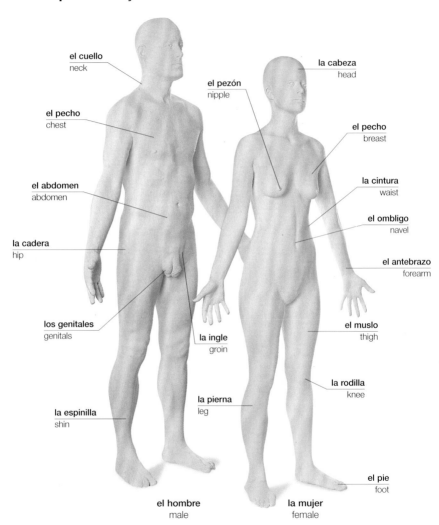

el cuello
neck

la cabeza
head

el pezón
nipple

el pecho
chest

el pecho
breast

la cintura
waist

el abdomen
abdomen

el ombligo
navel

la cadera
hip

el antebrazo
forearm

los genitales
genitals

la ingle
groin

el muslo
thigh

la rodilla
knee

la espinilla
shin

la pierna
leg

el pie
foot

el hombre
male

la mujer
female

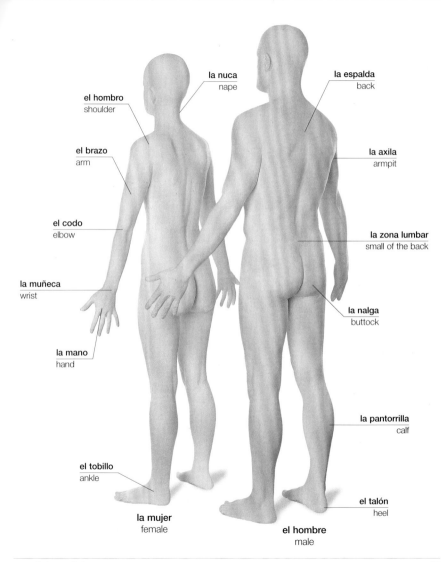

la nuca
nape

la espalda
back

el hombro
shoulder

la axila
armpit

el brazo
arm

el codo
elbow

la zona lumbar
small of the back

la muñeca
wrist

la nalga
buttock

la mano
hand

la pantorrilla
calf

el tobillo
ankle

el talón
heel

la mujer
female

el hombre
male

la cara • face

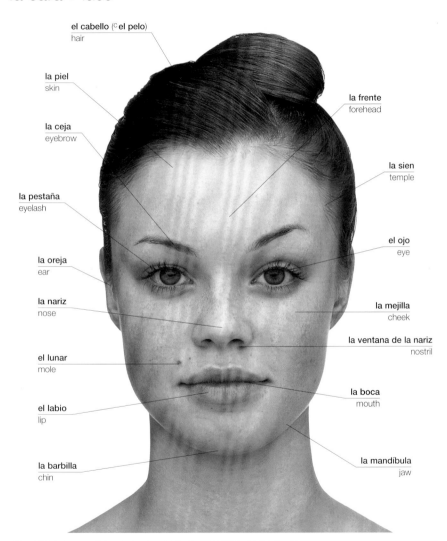

el cabello (ᶜel pelo)
hair

la piel
skin

la ceja
eyebrow

la pestaña
eyelash

la oreja
ear

la nariz
nose

el lunar
mole

el labio
lip

la barbilla
chin

la frente
forehead

la sien
temple

el ojo
eye

la mejilla
cheek

la ventana de la nariz
nostril

la boca
mouth

la mandíbula
jaw

la arruga
wrinkle

la peca
freckle

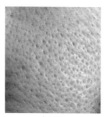

el poro
pore

el hoyuelo
dimple

la mano • hand

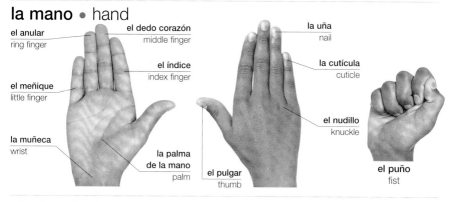

el anular
ring finger

el dedo corazón
middle finger

la uña
nail

el índice
index finger

la cutícula
cuticle

el meñique
little finger

la muñeca
wrist

el nudillo
knuckle

**la palma
de la mano**
palm

el pulgar
thumb

el puño
fist

el pie • foot

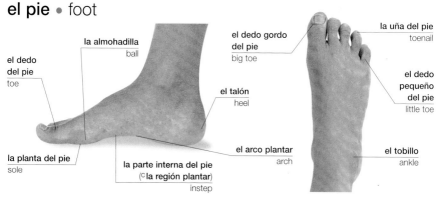

la almohadilla
ball

**el dedo gordo
del pie**
big toe

la uña del pie
toenail

**el dedo
del pie**
toe

el talón
heel

**el dedo
pequeño
del pie**
little toe

la planta del pie
sole

el arco plantar
arch

el tobillo
ankle

la parte interna del pie
(ᶜ**la región plantar**)
instep

los músculos • muscles

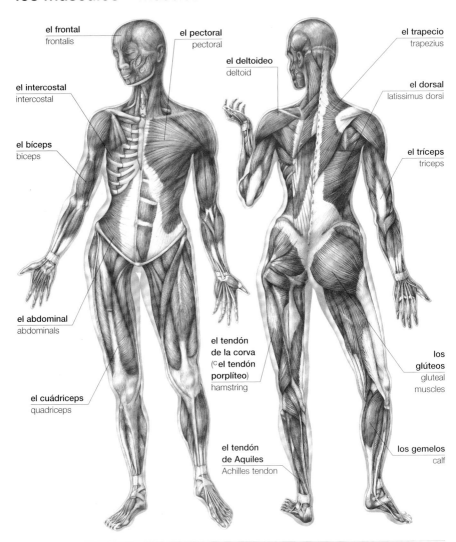

el frontal
frontalis

el pectoral
pectoral

el deltoideo
deltoid

el trapecio
trapezius

el intercostal
intercostal

el dorsal
latissimus dorsi

el bíceps
biceps

el tríceps
triceps

el abdominal
abdominals

el tendón
de la corva
(ᶜel tendón
porplíteo)
hamstring

los
glúteos
gluteal
muscles

el cuádriceps
quadriceps

el tendón
de Aquiles
Achilles tendon

los gemelos
calf

el esqueleto • skeleton

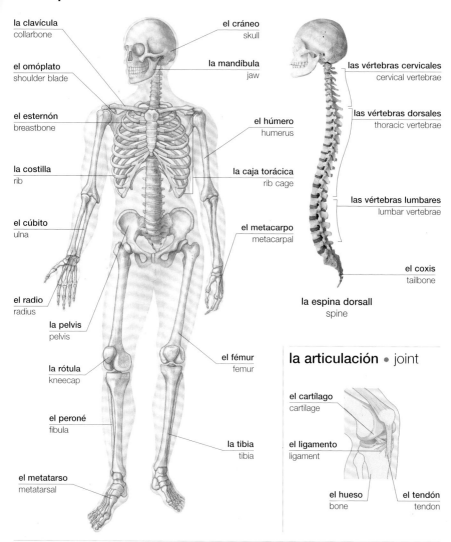

la clavícula
collarbone

el omóplato
shoulder blade

el esternón
breastbone

la costilla
rib

el cúbito
ulna

el radio
radius

la pelvis
pelvis

la rótula
kneecap

el peroné
fibula

el metatarso
metatarsal

el cráneo
skull

la mandíbula
jaw

el húmero
humerus

la caja torácica
rib cage

el metacarpo
metacarpal

el fémur
femur

la tibia
tibia

las vértebras cervicales
cervical vertebrae

las vértebras dorsales
thoracic vertebrae

las vértebras lumbares
lumbar vertebrae

el coxis
tailbone

la espina dorsall
spine

la articulación • joint

el cartílago
cartilage

el ligamento
ligament

el hueso
bone

el tendón
tendon

los órganos internos • internal organs

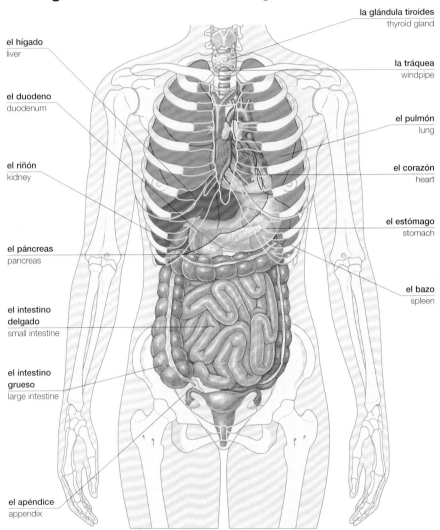

la glándula tiroides
thyroid gland

el hígado
liver

la tráquea
windpipe

el duodeno
duodenum

el pulmón
lung

el riñón
kidney

el corazón
heart

el estómago
stomach

el páncreas
pancreas

el bazo
spleen

el intestino
delgado
small intestine

el intestino
grueso
large intestine

el apéndice
appendix

la cabeza • head

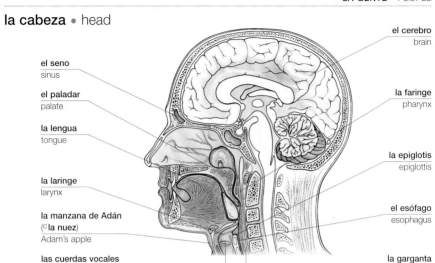

el cerebro
brain

el seno
sinus

el paladar
palate

la lengua
tongue

la faringe
pharynx

la epiglotis
epiglottis

la laringe
larynx

la manzana de Adán
(ᶜ la nuez)
Adam's apple

el esófago
esophagus

las cuerdas vocales
vocal cords

la garganta
throat

los sistemas • body systems

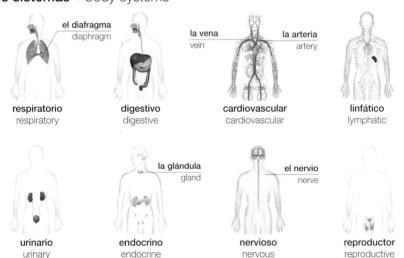

el diafragma
diaphragm

la vena
vein

la arteria
artery

respiratorio
respiratory

digestivo
digestive

cardiovascular
cardiovascular

linfático
lymphatic

la glándula
gland

el nervio
nerve

urinario
urinary

endocrino
endocrine

nervioso
nervous

reproductor
reproductive

los órganos reproductores
reproductive organs

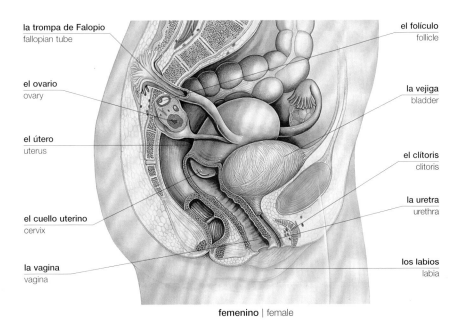

la trompa de Falopio
fallopian tube

el ovario
ovary

el útero
uterus

el cuello uterino
cervix

la vagina
vagina

el folículo
follicle

la vejiga
bladder

el clítoris
clitoris

la uretra
urethra

los labios
labia

femenino | female

la reproducción
reproduction

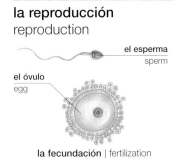

el esperma
sperm

el óvulo
egg

la fecundación | fertilization

vocabulario • vocabulary

la hormona hormone	**impotente** impotent	**la menstruación** menstruation
la ovulación ovulation	**fértil** fertile	**el coito** intercourse
estéril infertile	**concebir** conceive	**la infección de transmisión sexual** sexually transmitted infection

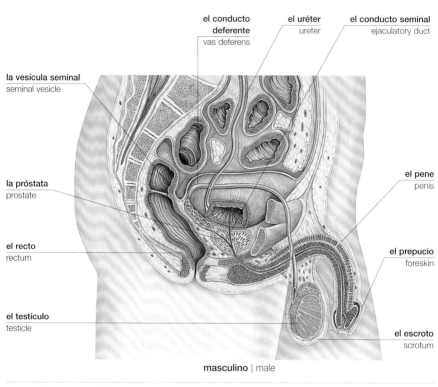

el conducto
deferente
vas deferens

el uréter
ureter

el conducto seminal
ejaculatory duct

la vesícula seminal
seminal vesicle

la próstata
prostate

el recto
rectum

el testículo
testicle

el pene
penis

el prepucio
foreskin

el escroto
scrotum

masculino | male

la anticoncepción • contraception

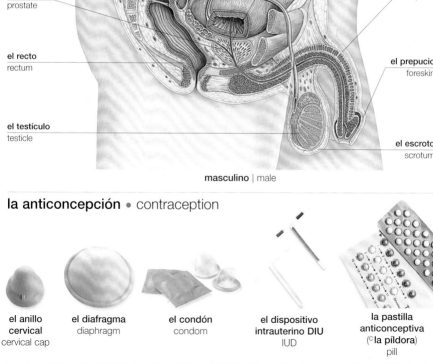

**el anillo
cervical**
cervical cap

el diafragma
diaphragm

el condón
condom

**el dispositivo
intrauterino DIU**
IUD

**la pastilla
anticonceptiva**
(^{c}**la píldora**)
pill

la familia • family

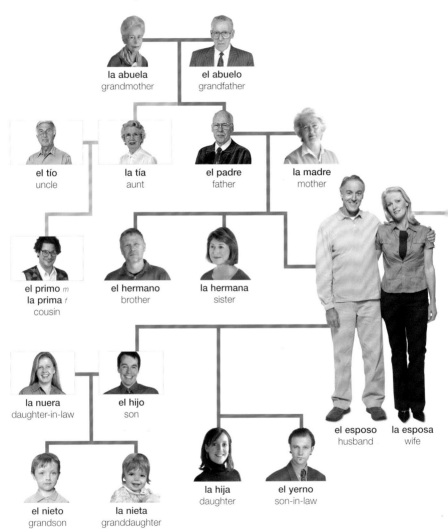

la abuela
grandmother

el abuelo
grandfather

el tío
uncle

la tía
aunt

el padre
father

la madre
mother

el primo *m*
la prima *f*
cousin

el hermano
brother

la hermana
sister

la nuera
daughter-in-law

el hijo
son

el esposo
husband

la esposa
wife

el nieto
grandson

la nieta
granddaughter

la hija
daughter

el yerno
son-in-law

vocabulario • vocabulary

los parientes relatives	**los padres** parents	**los nietos** m **las nietas** f grandchildren	**la madrastra** stepmother	**el hijastro** stepson	**la generación** generation
los abuelos grandparents	**los niños** m **las niñas** f children	**el padrastro** stepfather	**la hijastra** stepdaughter	**el compañero** m **la compañera** f partner	**los gemelos** m **las gemelas** f twins

la suegra
mother-in-law

el suegro
father-in-law

el cuñado
brother-in-law

la cuñada
sister-in-law

la sobrina
niece

el sobrino
nephew

los tratamientos
titles

Señor
Mr.

Señora
Mrs. / Ms.

Señorita
Miss

las etapas • stages

el bebé
baby

el niño m / **la niña** f
child

el niño
boy

la niña
girl

el adolescente m
la adolescente f
teenager

el adulto m
la adulta f
adult

el hombre
man

la mujer
woman

las relaciones • relationships

el jefe *m*
la jefe *f*
manager

el asistente *m*
la asistente *f*
(*c* **el ayudante** *m*
la ayudante *f*)
assistant

el socio *m*
la socia *f*
business
partner

el empleador *m*
la empleadora *f*
employer

el empleado *m*
la empleada *f*
employee

el compañero *m*
la compañera *f*
colleague

la oficina | office

el vecino *m* **/ la vecina** *f*
neighbor

el amigo *m* **/ la amiga** *f*
friend

el conocido *m*
la conocida *f*
acquaintance

**el amigo por
correspondencia** *m*
**la amiga por
correspondencia** *f*
pen pal

el novio
boyfriend

la novia
girlfriend

el prometido
fiancé

**la
prometida**
fiancée

la pareja | couple

la pareja prometida | engaged couple

las emociones • emotions

la sonrisa
smile

contento *m* / **contenta** *f*
happy

triste
sad

entusiasmado *m*
entusiasmada *f*
excited

aburrido *m*
aburrida *f*
bored

sorprendido *m*
sorprendida *f*
surprised

asustado *m* / **asustada** *f*
(ᶜ**atemorizado** *m* / **atemorizada** *f*)
scared

el ceño
fruncido
frown

enfadado *m* /
enfadada *f*
angry

confundido *m*
confundida *f*
confused

preocupado *m*
preocupada *f*
worried

nervioso *m*
nerviosa *f*
nervous

orgulloso *m*
orgullosa *f*
proud

confiado *m* / **confiada** *f*
(ᶜ**seguro** *m* / **segura** *f*)
confident

avergonzado *m*
avergonzada *f*
embarrassed

tímido *m*
tímida *f*
shy

vocabulario • vocabulary		
estupefacto *m* **estupefacta** *f* (ᶜ**impactado** *m* **impactada** *f*) shocked	**suspirar** sigh (v)	**llorar** cry (v)
	desmayarse faint (v)	**gritar** shout (v)
molesto *m* / **molesta** *f* (ᶜ**disgustado** *m* **disgustada** *f*) upset	**reír** laugh (v)	**bostezar** yawn (v)

los acontecimientos de una vida • life events

nacer
be born (v)

empezar el colegio
start school (v)

hacer amigos
make friends (v)

graduarse (ᶜlicenciarse)
graduate (v)

conseguir un trabajo
get a job (v)

enamorarse
fall in love (v)

casarse
get married (v)

tener un hijo
have a baby (v)

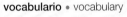

la boda | wedding

el divorcio
divorce

el funeral
funeral

vocabulario • vocabulary

el bautizo
christening

el bar mitzvah
bar mitzvah

el aniversario
anniversary

emigrar
emigrate (v)

jubilarse
retire (v)

morir
die (v)

hacer un testamento
make a will (v)

la celebración de la boda
wedding reception

la luna de miel
honeymoon

el acta (ᶜla partida) **de nacimiento**
birth certificate

las celebraciones • celebrations

las fiestas
festivals

la fiesta de
cumpleaños
birthday party

la tarjeta
card

el cumpleaños
birthday

el regalo
present

la Navidad
Christmas

la Pascua judía
Passover

el Año Nuevo
New Year

el carnaval
carnival

el desfile
procession

Fin del mes sagrado
de Ramadán
Eid

la cinta
ribbon

el Día de Acción de Gracias
Thanksgiving

la Pascua (ᶜ la
Semana Santa)
Easter

el día de Halloween
Halloween

el Diwali
Diwali

el aspecto
appearance

la ropa de niño • children's clothing

el bebé • baby

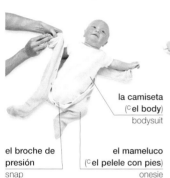

el traje de invierno (ᶜel buzo)
snowsuit

la camiseta
(ᶜel body)
bodysuit

el broche de
presión
snap

el mameluco
(ᶜel pelele con pies)
onesie

el mameluco
(ᶜel pijama enterizo)
sleeper

el mameluco (ᶜel
pelele) sin pies
romper

el babero
bib

los guantes
(ᶜlos manoplas)
mittens

las botas
(ᶜlos patucos)
booties

el pañal de tela
cloth diaper

el pañal
desechable
disposable diaper

el calzón (ᶜlas bra-
guitas) de plástico
plastic pants

el niño pequeño *m* / la niña pequeña *f* • toddler

la playera
(ᶜla camiseta)
T-shirt

los panatalones
con peto
overalls

el gorro para
el sol
sun hat

los shorts
(ᶜlos pantalones
cortos)
shorts

la falda
skirt

el delantal
apron

el niño *m* / la niña *f* • child

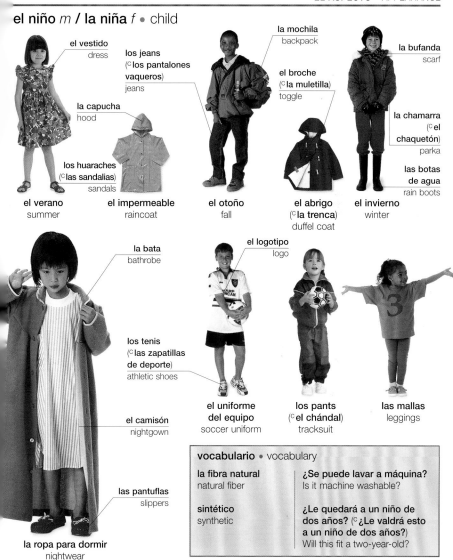

el vestido
dress

los jeans
(^C **los pantalones vaqueros**)
jeans

la capucha
hood

los huaraches
(^C **las sandalias**)
sandals

el verano
summer

el impermeable
raincoat

la mochila
backpack

el broche
(^C **la muletilla**)
toggle

el otoño
fall

el abrigo
(^C **la trenca**)
duffel coat

la bufanda
scarf

la chamarra
(^C **el chaquetón**)
parka

las botas de agua
rain boots

el invierno
winter

la bata
bathrobe

el logotipo
logo

los tenis
(^C **las zapatillas de deporte**)
athletic shoes

el camisón
nightgown

las pantuflas
slippers

la ropa para dormir
nightwear

el uniforme del equipo
soccer uniform

los pants
(^C **el chándal**)
tracksuit

las mallas
leggings

vocabulario • vocabulary

la fibra natural natural fiber	**¿Se puede lavar a máquina?** Is it machine washable?
sintético synthetic	**¿Le quedará a un niño de dos años?** (^C **¿Le valdrá esto a un niño de dos años?**) Will this fit a two-year-old?

la ropa • clothes (1)

el cuello
collar

la corbata
tie

el cinturón
belt

la solapa
lapel

el ojal
buttonhole

el puño
cuff

el bolsillo
pocket

la chaqueta
jacket

el botón
button

los pantalones
pants

el traje
(C el traje de chaqueta)
business suit

la gabardina
raincoat

el forro
lining

los zapatos
de piel
leather
shoes

---

vocabulario • vocabulary

el cardigan (C la rebeca) cardigan	la ropa interior underwear	la bata dressing gown	los pants (C el chándal) tracksuit
corto m corta f short	largo m larga f long	la gabardina (C el abrigo) coat	

¿Tiene una talla más grande / chica? (C¿Tiene una talla más / menos?)
Do you have this in a larger / smaller size?

¿Me lo puedo probar?
May I try this on?

el saco (^C**la chaqueta**)
blazer

el saco sport
(^C**la americana sport**)
sport coat

el chaleco
vest

el cuello en V
(^Cel cuello de pico)
V-neck

el cuello
redondo
crew neck

la camiseta
T-shirt

el chaquetón
parka

la sudadera
sweatshirt

la camisa
shirt

los tejanos
jeans

el suéter (^C**el jersey**)
sweater

la piyama (^C**el pijama**)
pajamas

la camiseta de tirantes
undershirt

la ropa informal
casual wear

los shorts (^C**los pantalones
cortos**) | shorts

los calzoncillos
briefs

los boxers (^C**los calzoncillos
de pata**) | boxer shorts

los calcetines
socks

la ropa • clothes (2)

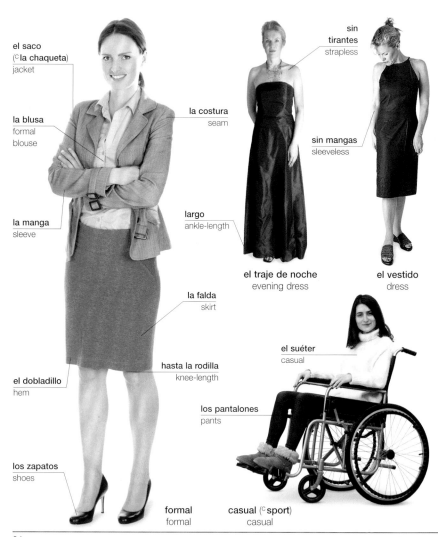

el saco
(ᶜla chaqueta)
jacket

la blusa
formal
blouse

la manga
sleeve

el dobladillo
hem

los zapatos
shoes

la costura
seam

largo
ankle-length

la falda
skirt

hasta la rodilla
knee-length

los pantalones
pants

sin
tirantes
strapless

sin mangas
sleeveless

el traje de noche
evening dress

el vestido
dress

el suéter
casual

formal
formal

casual (ᶜsport)
casual

la lencería • lingerie

el tirante
strap

la bata
robe

el fondo
(ᶜla combinación)
slip

la camisola
camisole

el liguero
garter straps

el corsé
bustier

la media
stocking

las pantimedias
(ᶜlas medias)
panty hose

el brasier
(ᶜel sujetador)
bra

las pantaletas
(ᶜlas bragas)
panties

el camisón
nightgown

la boda • wedding

el ramo
de flores
bouquet

el vestido de novia
wedding dress

vocabulario • vocabulary

el corsé corset	**el velo** veil
el brasier (ᶜsujetador) **deportivo** sports bra	**la liga** garter
con varillas (ᶜcon aros) underwire	**entallado** (ᶜsastre) tailored
la hombrera shoulder pad	**el cuello halter** halter neck
la cinturilla waistband	**el encaje** lace

los accesorios • accessories

la gorra
cap

el sombrero
hat

la bufanda
scarf

la hebilla
buckle

el cinturón
belt

el mango
(ᶜ el asa)
handle

la punta
tip

el pañuelo
handkerchief

el moño (ᶜ la pajarita)
bow tie

el alfiler de corbata
tiepin

los guantes
gloves

el paraguas
umbrella

las joyas • jewelry

el colguije
(ᶜ el colgante)
pendant

el prendedor
(ᶜ el broche)
brooch

las mancuernillas
(ᶜ el gemelo)
cuff links

el collar de perlas
strand of pearls

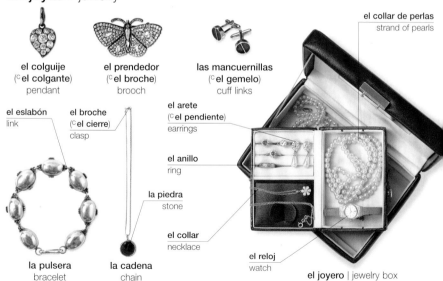

el eslabón
link

el broche
(ᶜ el cierre)
clasp

el arete
(ᶜ el pendiente)
earrings

el anillo
ring

la piedra
stone

el collar
necklace

el reloj
watch

la pulsera
bracelet

la cadena
chain

el joyero | jewelry box

los bolsos • bags

el cierre
clasp

la correa
shoulder strap

las asas
handles

la cartera
wallet

el monedero
change purse

la bolsa (^{c} el bolso)
shoulder bag

la bolsa de viaje
duffel bag

el maletín
briefcase

la bolsa (^{c} el bolso) **de mano**
handbag

la mochila
backpack

los zapatos • shoes

la agujeta
(^{c} el cordón)
lace

la lengüeta
tongue

el ojal
eyelet

el tacón
heel

la suela
sole

el zapato de agujetas
(^{c} de cordoneras)
lace-up

la bota de senderismo
hiking boot

el tenis (^{c} la zapatilla deportiva)
sneaker

la bota
boot

la chancla
flip-flop

el zapato de caballero
dress shoe

el zapato de tacón
high-heeled shoe

el zapato tacón de cuña (^{c} la cuña)
wedge

la sandalia
sandal

el mocasín
slip-on

la bailarina
flat

el cabello • hair

el peine
comb

peinar
comb (v)

el cepillo
brush

cepillar | brush (v)

el estilista m
la estilista f
(c **el peluquero** m
la peluquera f
hairdresser

el lavabo
sink

el cliente m
la clienta f
client

lavar | wash (v)

enjuagar
rinse (v)

cortar
cut (v)

la bata
robe

secar con la secadora (c **secar con el secador**) | blow-dry (v)

marcar
set (v)

los accesorios • accessories

la secadora
(c **el secador**)
blow-dryer

el champú
shampoo

el acondicionador (c **el suavizante**) | conditioner

el gel
gel

la laca
hairspray

las tenazas
(c **las tenacillas**)
curling iron

las tijeras
scissors

la diadema
headband

la plancha de pelo
hair straightener

el pasador (c **la horquilla**) | bobby pins

los estilos • styles

la cola de caballo
ponytail

la trenza
braid

el chongo (ᶜ **el moño) francés**
French twist

el chongo
(ᶜ **el moño)**
bun

las coletas
pigtails

el príncipe valiente
(ᶜ **la melena) | bob**

el pelo corto
short haircut

rizado
curly

la permanente
perm

lacio
straight

las raíces
roots

las luces (ᶜ **los reflejos)**
highlights

calvo
bald

la peluca
wig

vocabulario • vocabulary

lla goma del pelo hair tie	**graso** greasy
cortar las puntas trim (v)	**seco** dry
alisar straighten (v)	**normal** normal
las puntas abiertas split ends	**el cuero cabelludo** scalp
el barbero barber	**la barba** beard
la caspa dandruff	**el bigote** mustache

los colores • colors

güero (ᶜ **rubio)**
blond / blonde

castaño
brunette

rojizo
auburn

pelirrojo
red

negro
black

gris
gray

blanco
white

teñido
dyed

la belleza • beauty

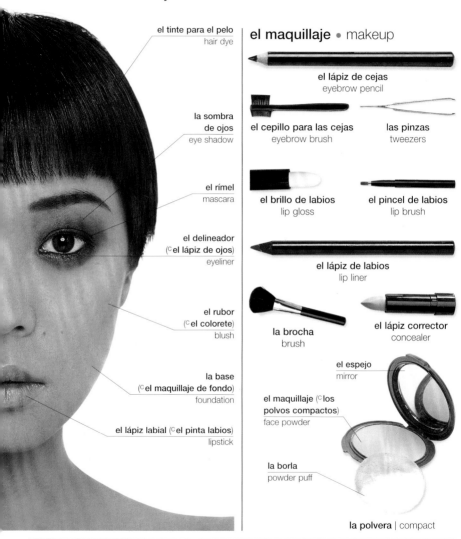

el tinte para el pelo
hair dye

la sombra
de ojos
eye shadow

el rímel
mascara

el delineador
(ᶜel lápiz de ojos)
eyeliner

el rubor
(ᶜel colorete)
blush

la base
(ᶜel maquillaje de fondo)
foundation

el lápiz labial (ᶜel pinta labios)
lipstick

el maquillaje • makeup

el lápiz de cejas
eyebrow pencil

el cepillo para las cejas
eyebrow brush

las pinzas
tweezers

el brillo de labios
lip gloss

el pincel de labios
lip brush

el lápiz de labios
lip liner

la brocha
brush

el lápiz corrector
concealer

el espejo
mirror

el maquillaje (ᶜlos
polvos compactos)
face powder

la borla
powder puff

la polvera | compact

los tratamientos de belleza
beauty treatments

la mascarilla
face mask

la depilación con hilo
threading

la limpieza de cutis
facial

exfoliar
exfoliate (v)

la depilación a la cera
wax

la pedicura
pedicure

los artículos de tocador
toiletries

la crema (ᶜ la leche) limpiadora
cleanser

el tónico
toner

la crema hidratante
moisturizer

la crema bronceadora
(ᶜ autobronceadora)
self-tanning lotion

el perfume
perfume

el agua de colonia
eau de toilette

la manicura • manicure

el quitaesmalte
nail polish remover

la lima de uñas
nail file

el esmalte de uñas
nail polish

las tijeras de uñas
nail scissors

el cortaúñas
nail clippers

vocabulario • vocabulary

el cutis complexion	**sensible** sensitive	**antiarrugas** antiwrinkle
claro fair	**hipoalergénico** **hipoalergénica** hypoallergenic	**las bolas de algodón** cotton balls
moreno dark	**el tono** shade	**la manteca de cacao** cocoa butter
seco dry	**el bronceado** tan	
graso oily	**el tatuaje** tattoo	

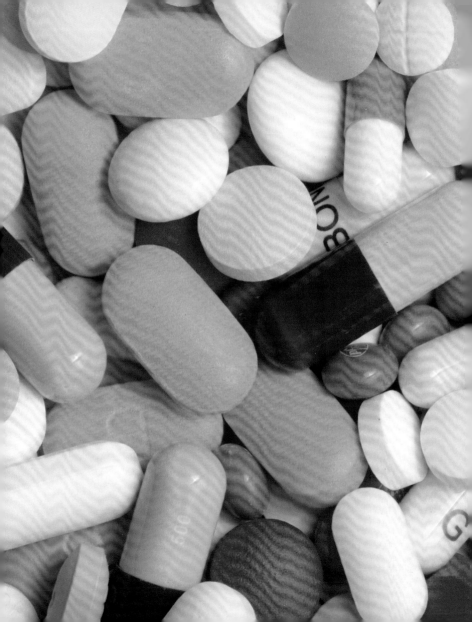

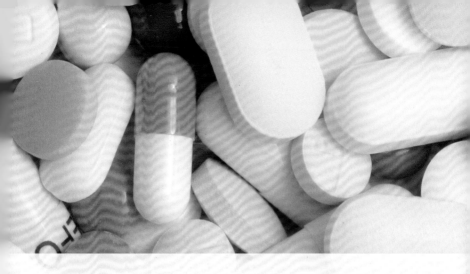

la salud
health

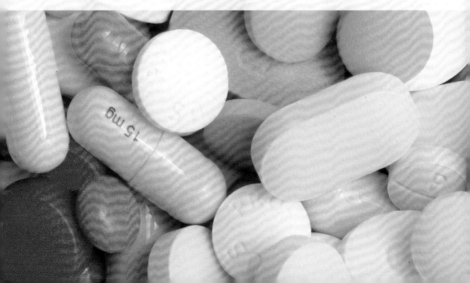

la enfermedad • illness

la fiebre | fever

el dolor de cabeza
headache

la hemorragia nasal
nosebleed

la tos
cough

el estornudo
sneeze

el resfriado
cold

la gripe
flu

el inhalador
inhaler

el asma
asthma

los calambres
cramps

la náusea
nausea

la varicela
chicken pox

el sarpullido
rash

---

vocabulario • vocabulary

la aplopejía (ᶜel derrame cerebral) stroke	**la fiebre del heno** hay fever	**la infección** infection	**el dolor de estómago** stomachache	**la migraña (ᶜla jaqueca)** migraine	**la diarrea** diarrhea
la diabetes diabetes	**la alergia** allergy	**el eccema** eczema	**el resfriado** chill	**vomitar** vomit (v)	**el sarampión** measles
el ataque cardiaco (ᶜel infarto de miocardio) heart attack	**la presión arterial (ᶜla tensión arterial)** blood pressure	**el virus** virus	**desmayarse** faint (v)	**la epilepsia** epilepsy	**las paperas** mumps

el doctor *m* / la doctora *f* • doctor
la consulta • consultation

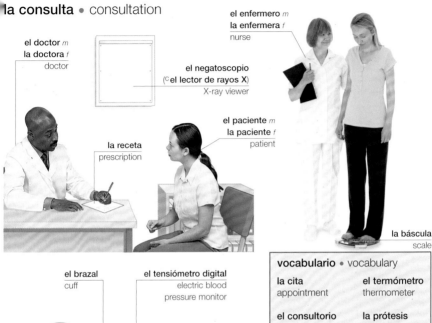

el doctor *m*
la doctora *f*
doctor

el negatoscopio
(ᶜ el lector de rayos X)
X-ray viewer

el enfermero *m*
la enfermera *f*
nurse

la receta
prescription

el paciente *m*
la paciente *f*
patient

la báscula
scale

el brazal
cuff

el tensiómetro digital
electric blood
pressure monitor

---

vocabulario • vocabulary

la cita
appointment

el consultorio
doctor's office

la sala de espera
waiting room

la inoculación
vaccination

el termómetro
thermometer

**la prótesis
auditiva**
(ᶜ **el audífono**)
hearing aid

**el examen
médico**
medical
examination

Necesito ver a un médico.
I need to see a doctor.

Me duele aquí.
It hurts here.

la lesión • injury

la torcedura | sprain

el cabestrillo
sling

la fractura
fracture

el collarín
neck brace

el tirón en el cuello
whiplash

la cortada (ᶜel corte)
cut

la raspada (ᶜel arañazo)
graze

el moretón (ᶜel hematoma)
bruise

la astilla
splinter

la ardida (ᶜla
quemadura de sol)
sunburn

la quemadura
burn

el mordisco
bite

la picadura
sting

vocabulario • vocabulary

el accidente accident	**la hemorragia** hemorrhage	**el shock eléctrico** (ᶜla descarga eléctrica) electric shock	¿Se pondrá bien? Will he / she be all right?
la herida wound	**la ampolla** blister		**Por favor llame a una ambulancia.** Please call an ambulance.
la emergencia (ᶜla urgencia) emergency	**la lesión en la cabeza** head injury	**el envenenamiento** poisoning	¿Dónde le duele? Where does it hurt?
		la conmoción cerebral concussion	

los primeros auxilios • first aid

la pomada
ointment

la tirita
adhesive
bandage

el seguro
(C el imperdible)
safety pin

la venda
bandage

los analgésicos
painkillers

la toallita
antiséptica
antiseptic wipe

las pinzas
tweezers

las tijeras
scissors

el desinfectante
antiseptic

el botiquín | first-aid kit

la gasa
gauze

el vendaje
dressing

la tablilla | splint

la tela adhesiva
(C el esparadrapo)
adhesive tape

la reanimación
resuscitation

vocabulario • vocabulary			
el shock shock	el pulso pulse	ahogarse choke (v)	¿Me puede ayudar? Can you help me?
inconsciente unconscious	la respiración breathing	estéril sterile	¿Sabe primeros auxilios? Do you know first aid?

el hospital • hospital

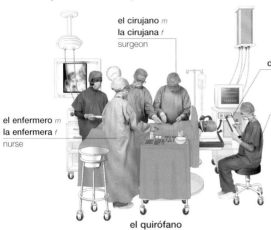

el cirujano *m*
la cirujana *f*
surgeon

el historial
médico
(ᶜla gráfica
del paciente)
chart

el enfermero *m*
la enfermera *f*
nurse

el anestesista *m*
la anestesista *f*
anesthesiologist

el quirófano
operating room

el análisis de sangre
blood test

la inyección
injection

la radiografía
X-ray

la camilla
gurney

la sala de urgencias
emergency room

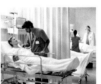

la planta
ward

la silla de ruedas
wheelchair

el ultrasonido
(ᶜla ecografía)
scan

---

vocabulario • vocabulary

internado *m*	dado de alta *m*	la clínica	la sala de	la habitación	el paciente
internada *f*	dada de alta *f*	clinic	pediatría	privada	externo *m*
(ᶜingresado *m*	discharged		children's ward	private room	la paciente
ingresada *f*)		las horas de			externa *f*
admitted	la operación	visita	la sala de	la unidad de	outpatient
	operation	visiting hours	maternidad	cuidados intensivos	
			maternity ward	intensive care unit	

los servicios • departments

la otorrinolaringología
ENT

la cardiología
cardiology

la ortopedia
orthopedics

la ginecología
gynecology

la fisioterapia
physiotherapy

la dermatología
dermatology

la pediatría
pediatrics

la radiología
radiology

la cirugía
surgery

la maternidad
maternity

la psiquiatría
psychiatry

la oftalmología
ophthalmology

---

vocabulario • vocabulary

la neurología neurology	**la urología** urology	**la cirugía plástica** plastic surgery	**la patología** pathology	**el resultado** result
la oncología oncology	**la endocrinología** endocrinology	**la referencia** (ᶜ **el volante**) referral	**el análisis** test	**el especialista** *m* **la especialista** *f* specialist

el dentista *m* / la dentista *f* • dentist

el diente • tooth

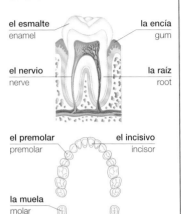

el esmalte
enamel

la encía
gum

el nervio
nerve

la raíz
root

el premolar
premolar

el incisivo
incisor

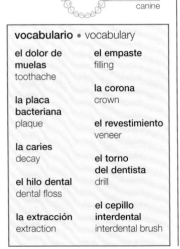

la muela
molar

el colmillo
canine

vocabulario • vocabulary

el dolor de
muelas
toothache

el empaste
filling

la placa
bacteriana
plaque

la corona
crown

la caries
decay

el revestimiento
veneer

el hilo dental
dental floss

el torno
del dentista
drill

la extracción
extraction

el cepillo
interdental
interdental brush

la revisión • checkup

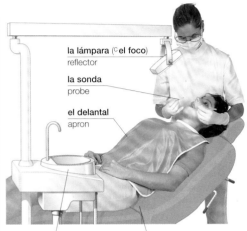

la lámpara (^C el foco)
reflector

la sonda
probe

el delantal
apron

el lavabo
sink

el sillón del dentista
dentist's chair

usar el
hilo dental
floss (v)

cepillarse los
dientes
brush (v)

los frenos (^C el
aparato corrector)
braces

la radiografía
dental
dental X-ray

la radiografía
X-ray film

la dentadura
postiza
dentures

el optometrista *m* / la optometrista *f* • optometrist

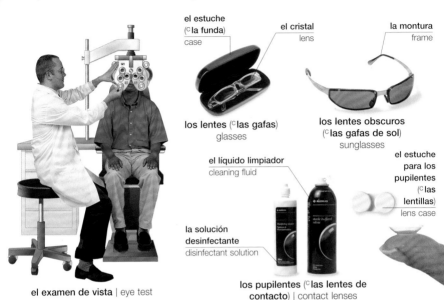

el estuche
(^Cla funda)
case

el cristal
lens

la montura
frame

los lentes (^Clas gafas)
glasses

los lentes obscuros
(^Clas gafas de sol)
sunglasses

el líquido limpiador
cleaning fluid

el estuche
para los
pupilentes
(^Clas
lentillas)
lens case

la solución
desinfectante
disinfectant solution

el examen de vista | eye test

los pupilentes (^Clas lentes de
contacto) | contact lenses

el ojo • eye

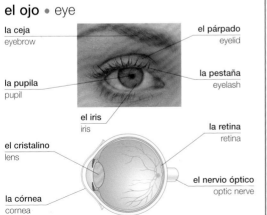

la ceja
eyebrow

el párpado
eyelid

la pupila
pupil

la pestaña
eyelash

el iris
iris

el cristalino
lens

la retina
retina

la córnea
cornea

el nervio óptico
optic nerve

vocabulario • vocabulary	
la vista vision	el astigmatismo astigmatism
la dioptría diopter	la hipermetropía farsighted
la lágrima tear	la miopía nearsighted
la catarata cataract	bifocal bifocal
ciego *m* ciega *f* blind	el glaucoma glaucoma

el embarazo • pregnancy

la prueba del embarazo
pregnancy test

el ultrasonido
(^{C} la ecografía)
scan

el cordón
umbilical
umbilical cord

la placenta
placenta

el cuello
uterino
cervix

el útero
uterus

el ultrasonido | ultrasound

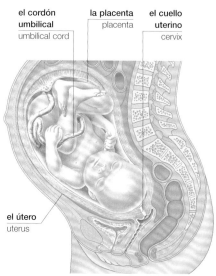

el feto | fetus

---

vocabulario • vocabulary

la ovulación ovulation	el embrión embryo	la dilatación dilation	la episiotomía episiotomy	prematuro premature	el ginecólogo *m* la ginecóloga *f* gynecologist
la concepción conception	la matriz womb	prenatal prenatal	de espaldas (^{C} el parto de nalgas) breech birth	las puntadas (^{C} los puntos) stitches	el obstetra *m* la obstetra *f* obstetrician
embarazada / encinta pregnant / expecting	la contracción contraction	la epidural epidural	el aborto espontáneo miscarriage	la leche de fórmula baby formula	¡He roto aguas! My water broke!
el trimestre trimester	el líquido amniótico amniotic fluid	el parto delivery	el nacimiento birth	dar el biberón bottle-feed (v)	
	la amniocentesis amniocentesis	la cesárea cesarean section			

---

el parto • childbirth

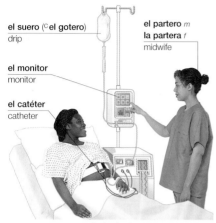

el suero (^cel gotero)
drip

el partero *m*
la partera *f*
midwife

el monitor
monitor

el catéter
catheter

inducir el parto
induce labor (v)

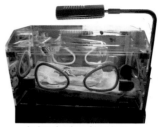

la incubadora | incubator

el peso al nacer
birth weight

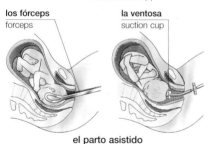

los fórceps
forceps

la ventosa
suction cup

el parto asistido
assisted delivery

la pulsera de identificación
identity tag

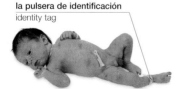

el recién nacido *m* / la recién nacida *f*
newborn baby

la lactancia • nursing

el tiraleches
(^cel sacaleches)
breast pump

el brasier
(^cel sujetador)
para la lactancia
nursing bra

amamantar
(^cdar el pecho)
breastfeed (v)

los discos protectores
de lactancia
nursing pads

las terapias complementarias • complementary therapies

la postura de yoga
yoga pose

la colchoneta
mat

el yoga | yoga

el masaje
massage

el shiatsu
shiatsu

la quiropráctica
chiropractic

la osteopatía
osteopathy

la reflexología
reflexology

la meditación
meditation

el psicólogo _m_
la psicóloga _f_
counselor

la terapia de grupo
group therapy

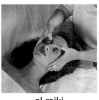

el reiki
reiki

la acupuntura
acupuncture

la ayurveda
ayurveda

la hipnoterapia
hypnotherapy

los aceites esenciales
essential oils

el herbolario
herbalism

la aromaterapia
aromatherapy

la homeopatía
homeopathy

la acupresión
acupressure

el terapeuta _m_
la terapeuta _f_
therapist

la psicoterapia
psychotherapy

vocabulario • vocabulary			
la cristaloterapia crystal healing	**la naturopatía** naturopathy	**la relajación** relaxation	**de hierbas** herbal
la hidroterapia hydrotherapy	**el feng shui** feng shui	**el estrés** stress	**el suplemento** supplement

la casa
home

la casa • house

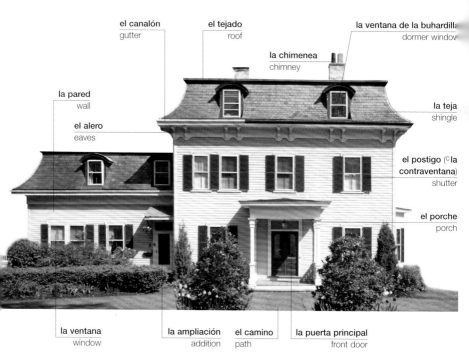

el canalón
gutter

el tejado
roof

la ventana de la buhardilla
dormer window

la chimenea
chimney

la pared
wall

el alero
eaves

la teja
shingle

el postigo (^Cla contraventana)
shutter

el porche
porch

la ventana
window

la ampliación
addition

el camino
path

la puerta principal
front door

---

vocabulario • vocabulary

la casa adosada row house	dúplex (^Cla casa pareada) duplex	la cochera (^Cel garaje) garage	la luz del porche porch light	la alarma antirrobo burglar alarm	la renta (^Cel alquiler) rent
la casa independiente single-family	el sótano basement	el ático attic	el piso floor	el propietario m la propietaria f landlord	rentar (^Calquilar) rent (v)
la vivienda urbana townhouse	el bungalow bungalow	el cuarto (^Cla habitación) room	el patio courtyard	el inquilino m la inquilina f tenant	el buzón mailbox

la entrada • entrance

el departamento (^C el piso)
apartment

el balcón
balcony

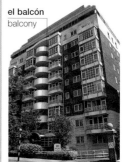

el edificio
apartment building

el pasamanos
hand rail

el descanso
(^C el descansillo)
landing

el barandal
(^C la barandilla)
banister

la escalera
staircase

el vestíbulo
foyer

el interfono
intercom

el timbre
doorbell

el tapete (^C el felpudo)
doormat

la aldaba
door knocker

la llave
key

la cadena
door chain

la cerradura
lock

el cerrojo
bolt

el elevador (^C el ascensor)
elevator

las instalaciones internas · internal systems

el aspa
blade

el ventilador
fan

el radiador
radiator

el calentador (ᶜla estufa)
space heater

el calentador
de convección
convection heater

la electricidad · electricity

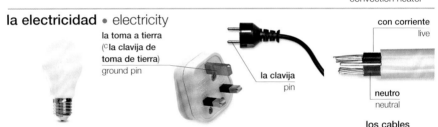

la toma a tierra
(ᶜla clavija de
toma de tierra)
ground pin

con corriente
live

la clavija
pin

neutro
neutral

la bombilla de ahorro de energía
energy-saving bulb

el enchufe
plug

los cables
wires

vocabulario · vocabulary

el voltaje voltage	el generador generator	el enchufe outlet	la corriente continua direct current	el transformador transformer
el amperio amp	el fusible fuse	el interruptor switch	el contador de la luz electric meter	el suministro de electricidad household current
la corriente eléctrica power	la caja de fusibles fuse box	la corriente alterna alternating current	el corte de luz power outage	

la fontanería • plumbing

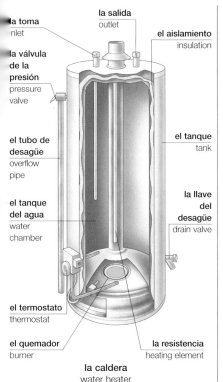

la toma
inlet

la salida
outlet

el aislamiento
insulation

la válvula
de la
presión
pressure
valve

el tubo de
desagüe
overflow
pipe

el tanque
del agua
water
chamber

el termostato
thermostat

el quemador
burner

el tanque
tank

la llave
del
desagüe
drain valve

la resistencia
heating element

la caldera
water heater

el fregador • sink

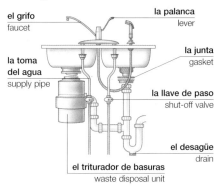

el grifo
faucet

la palanca
lever

la toma
del agua
supply pipe

la junta
gasket

la llave de paso
shut-off valve

el desagüe
drain

el triturador de basuras
waste disposal unit

el excusado (ᶜ el váter) • toilet

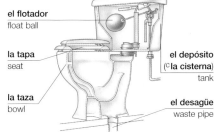

el flotador
float ball

la tapa
seat

la taza
bowl

el depósito
(ᶜ la cisterna)
tank

el desagüe
waste pipe

la eliminación de desechos • waste disposal

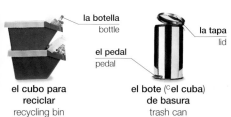

la botella
bottle

la tapa
lid

el pedal
pedal

el cubo para
reciclar
recycling bin

el bote (ᶜ el cuba)
de basura
trash can

el cajón para
clasificar basura
sorting bin

los desperdicios
orgánicos
organic waste

la sala (^Cel cuarto de estar) • living room

el arbotante
(^Cel aplique)
wall light

la chimenea
fireplace

el techo
ceiling

la lámpara
lamp

el jarrón
vase

el cojín
pillow

la mesa
de centro
(^Cla mesa
de café)
coffee table

el sofá
sofa

el piso
(^Cel suelo)
floor

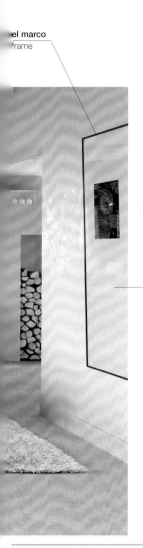

el marco
frame

el cuadro
picture

la cortina
curtain

el visillo
sheer curtain

la persiana (ᶜel estor
de láminas)
Venetian blind

el estor
roller blind

la moldura
molding

el sillón
armchair

el librero
(ᶜla estantería)
bookshelf

el sofá-cama
sofa bed

el tapete
(ᶜla alfombra)
rug

el estudio (ᶜel despacho) | study

el comedor • dining room

la pimienta
pepper

la sal
salt

la mesa
table

la vajilla
crockery

los cubiertos
cutlery

la silla
chair

el respaldo
back

el asiento
seat

la pata
leg

vocabulario • vocabulary

servir serve (v)	la comida meal	el desayuno breakfast	hambriento *m* hambrienta *f* hungry	el anfitrión *m* host	**Estaba riquísimo.** (ᶜ**Estaba buenísimo.**) That was delicious.
comer eat (v)	el mantel tablecloth	la comida lunch	lleno *m* llena *f* full	la anfitriona *f* hostess	**Estoy satisfecho, gracias.** I've had enough, thank you.
poner la mesa set the table (v)	el mantel individual placemat	la cena dinner	la ración portion	el invitado *m* la invitada *f* guest	**¿Puedo comer otro poco?** (ᶜ**¿Puedo repetir, por favor?**) Can I have some more, please?

la vajilla y los cubiertos • crockery and cutlery

la taza
mug

la taza de café
coffee cup

la cucharilla de café
teaspoon

la taza de té
teacup

el plato
plate

el plato sopero
(ᶜ**el bol**)
bowl

la prensa francesa
(ᶜ**la cafetera de
émbolo**)
French press

la tetera
teapot

la jarra
pitcher

la copa de vino
wine glass

el vaso
tumbler

la taza para el huevo
(ᶜ**la huevera**)
eggcup

la cristalería
glassware

el servilletero
napkin ring

**el plato
del pan**
side plate

el plato
(ᶜ**el plato llano**)
dinner plate

**el plato
sopero**
soup bowl

la cuchara sopera
soup spoon

la servilleta
napkin

el tenedor
fork

el lugar en la mesa
place setting

la cuchara
spoon

el cuchillo
knife

la cocina • kitchen

el estante
shelf

la pared de
azulejo
(^{C} el frente de
la cocina)
backsplash

el grifo
faucet

el fregadero
sink

el cajón
drawer

el extractor
ventilation hood

la placa
vitrocerámica
ceramic
stovetop

la encimera
countertop

el horno
oven

la gaveta
(^{C} el armario)
cabinet

los electrodomésticos • appliances

el (^{C} horno) microondas
microwave oven

el recipiente (^{C} el
cuenco mezclador)
mixing bowl

la cuchilla
blade

la tapa
lid

la jarra para hervir
(^{C} el hervidor)
electric kettle

el tostador
toaster

el procesador de alimentos
(^{C} el robot de cocina)
food processor

la licuadora
blender

la lavavajilla
(^{C} el friegaplatos)
dishwasher

la máquina de los hielos
ice maker

el refrigerador
(ᶜ **el frigorífico**)
refrigerator

el congelador
freezer

el cajón de las verduras
crisper

el refrigerador (ᶜ **frigorífico**) **congelador**
side-by-side refrigerator

vocabulario • vocabulary

el quemador
burner

la hornilla
(ᶜ **la placa**)
stovetop

el escurridor
draining board

congelar
freeze (v)

el bote de basura
(ᶜ **el cubo de basura**)
garbage can

descongelar
defrost (v)

cocer al vapor
steam (v)

saltear
sauté (v)

cocinar • cooking

pelar
peel (v)

cortar
slice (v)

rallar
grate (v)

vaciar (ᶜ **echar**)
pour (v)

mezclar
mix (v)

batir
whisk (v)

hervir
boil (v)

freír
fry (v)

amasar (ᶜ **extender**)
con el rodillo | roll (v)

remover
stir (v)

cocer a fuego lento
simmer (v)

escalfar
poach (v)

hornear
(ᶜ **cocer al horno**)
bake (v)

asar
roast (v)

asar a la parrilla
broil (v)

los utensilios de cocina • kitchenware

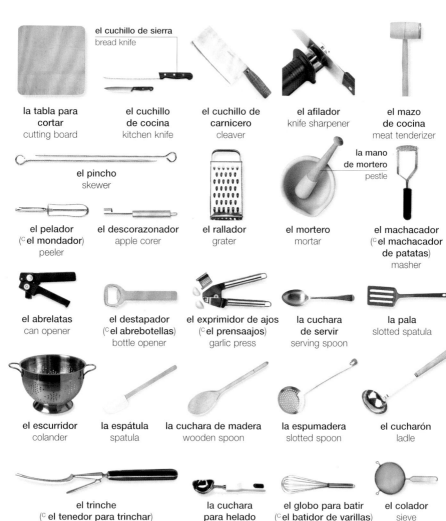

la tabla para cortar
cutting board

el cuchillo de sierra
bread knife

el cuchillo de cocina
kitchen knife

el cuchillo de carnicero
cleaver

el afilador
knife sharpener

el mazo de cocina
meat tenderizer

el pincho
skewer

el pelador
(ᶜ **el mondador**)
peeler

el descorazonador
apple corer

el rallador
grater

la mano de mortero
pestle

el mortero
mortar

el machacador
(ᶜ **el machacador de patatas**)
masher

el abrelatas
can opener

el destapador
(ᶜ **el abrebotellas**)
bottle opener

el exprimidor de ajos
(ᶜ **el prensaajos**)
garlic press

la cuchara de servir
serving spoon

la pala
slotted spatula

el escurridor
colander

la espátula
spatula

la cuchara de madera
wooden spoon

la espumadera
slotted spoon

el cucharón
ladle

el trinche
(ᶜ **el tenedor para trinchar**)
carving fork

la cuchara para helado
ice-cream scoop

el globo para batir
(ᶜ **el batidor de varillas**)
whisk

el colador
sieve

la tapa
lid

antiadherente
nonstick

la sartén
frying pan

la cacerola
(ᶜ**el cazo**)
saucepan

la parrilla
grill pan

el wok
wok

el tajine
tagine

de cristal
glass

resistente al horno
ovenproof

la ensaladera
(ᶜ**el cuenco**)
mixing bowl

el molde para suflé
soufflé dish

**la fuente
para gratinar**
gratin dish

**el molde
individual**
ramekin

la cazuela
casserole dish

la repostería • baking cakes

**la báscula
de cocina**
scale

la taza medidora
(ᶜ**la jarra graduada**)
measuring cup

**el molde para
pastel** (ᶜ**bizcocho**)
cake pan

el molde redondo
pie pan

el molde para pie
(ᶜ**la flanera**)
quiche pan

la brocha de cocina
pastry brush

el rodillo de cocina
rolling pin

la dulla (ᶜ**la manga pastelera**)
piping bag

**el molde para
panqués**
(ᶜ**magdalenas**)
muffin pan

la charola (ᶜ **la
bandeja**) **de horno**
cookie sheet

la rejilla
cooling rack

el guante (ᶜ**la
manopla**) **de cocina**
oven mitt

el delantal
apron

la recámara (^C el dormitorio) • bedroom

el armario
closet

la lámpara
del buró
(^C de la mesilla)
bedside lamp

la cabecera
(^C el cabecero)
headboard

el buró
(^C la mesilla
de noche)
nightstand

la cómoda
chest of drawers

el cajón	la cama	el colchón	la colcha	la almohada
drawer	bed	mattress	bedspread	pillow

la bolsa de
agua caliente
hot-water bottle

la radio
despertador
clock radio

el reloj
despertador
alarm clock

la caja de pañuelos
desechables
box of tissues

el gancho
(^C la percha)
coat hanger

la ropa de cama • bed linen

el espejo
mirror

el tocador
dressing
table

**la funda de
la almohada**
pillowcase

la sábana
sheet

el edredón
comforter

la colcha
quilt

la cobija
(ᶜla manta)
blanket

el suelo
floor

---

vocabulario • vocabulary

la cama individual twin bed	**el pie de la cama** footboard	**el insomnio** insomnia	**despertarse** wake up (v)	**roncar** snore (v)
la cama matrimonial (ᶜde matrimonio) full bed	**el resorte** (ᶜel somier) bedspring	**acostarse** go to bed (v)	**levantarse** get up (v)	**poner el despertador** set the alarm (v)
		dormirse go to sleep (v)	**hacer la cama** make the bed (v)	
la cobija (ᶜla manta) **eléctrica** electric blanket	**el tapete** (ᶜla moqueta) carpet			**el armario empotrado** closet

---

el cuarto de baño • bathroom

el toallero
towel rack

la puerta de la regadera (ᶜducha)
shower door

la llave (ᶜel grifo) de agua fría
cold faucet

la llave (ᶜel grifo) de agua caliente
hot faucet

la piña de la regadera (ᶜla alcachofa de la ducha)
shower head

el lavabo
sink

el tapón
plug

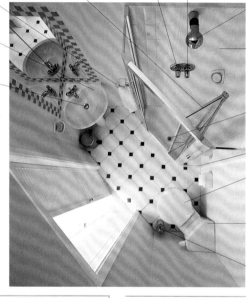

la regadera (ᶜla ducha)
shower

el desagüe
drain

el asiento del excusado (ᶜla tapa del váter)
toilet seat

el excusado (ᶜel váter)
toilet

la escobilla del excusado (ᶜdel váter)
toilet brush

la tina (ᶜla bañera)
bathtub

el bidé | bidet

---

vocabulario • vocabulary

el botiquín (ᶜel armario de las medicinas)
medicine cabinet

el tapete (ᶜla alfombrilla de baño)
bath mat

el rollo de papel higiénico
toilet paper

la cortina de la regadera (ᶜde ducha)
shower curtain

bañarse (ᶜdarse una ducha)
take a shower (v)

darse un baño
take a bath (v)

la higiene dental • dental hygiene

el cepillo de dientes
toothbrush

el hilo dental
dental floss

la pasta de dientes
toothpaste

el enjuague bucal
mouthwash

la esponja
sponge

la piedra pómez
pumice stone

**el cepillo para
la espalda**
back brush

el desodorante
deodorant

la jabonera
soap dish

el shampoo para el cuerpo
(C el gel de ducha)
shower gel

el jabón
soap

la crema para la cara
face cream

el gel de baño
bubble bath

la toalla de mano
(C de lavabo)
hand towel

**la toalla
de baño**
bath towel

las toallas
towels

la crema para el cuerpo
(C la leche corporal)
body lotion

el talco (C los
polvos de talco)
talcum powder

la bata
(C el albornoz)
bathrobe

el afeitado • shaving

la rasuradora
(C la maquinilla
eléctrica)
electric razor

la espuma de afeitar
shaving foam

la navaja de afeitar desechable
(C la cuchilla de afeitar
desechable) | disposable razor

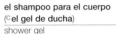
**la hoja
de afeitar**
razor blade

el aftershave
aftershave

la habitación del bebé • nursery

el cuidado del bebé • baby care

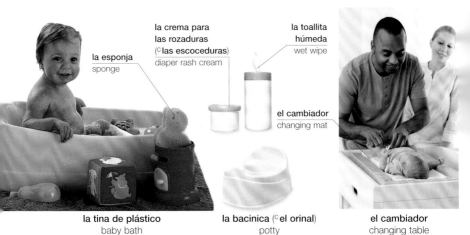

la crema para
las rozaduras
(ᶜ las escoceduras)
diaper rash cream

la esponja
sponge

la toallita
húmeda
wet wipe

el cambiador
changing mat

la tina de plástico
baby bath

la bacinica (ᶜ **el orinal**)
potty

el cambiador
changing table

la hora de dormir • sleeping

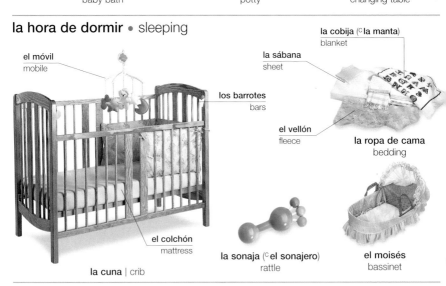

el móvil
mobile

los barrotes
bars

la cobija (ᶜ la manta)
blanket

la sábana
sheet

el vellón
fleece

la ropa de cama
bedding

el colchón
mattress

la cuna | crib

la sonaja (ᶜ **el sonajero**)
rattle

el moisés
bassinet

os juegos • playing

la muñeca
doll

el muñeco de peluche
stuffed toy

la casa de muñecas
dollhouse

la casa de juguete
playhouse

el oso de peluche
teddy bear

el juguete
toy

el cesto de los juguetes
toy basket

la pelota
ball

el corral (ᶜ**el parque**)
playpen

la seguridad
safety

**el cierre
de seguridad**
child lock

el monitor del bebé
baby monitor

**la barrera de
seguridad**
stair gate

la comida
eating

la periquera (ᶜ**la trona**)
high chair

el chupón
(ᶜ**la tetina**)
nipple

la mamila
(ᶜ**el biberón**)
bottle

la taza
sippy cup

el paseo • going out

la carriola
(ᶜ**la silleta de paseo**)
stroller

la carriola
(ᶜ**el cochecito de niños**)
baby carriage

la capota
hood

el bambineto (ᶜ**el
capazo**) | carrier

el pañal
diaper

la pañalera (ᶜ**la bolsa
del bebé**) | diaper bag

la cangurera (ᶜ**la mochila
de bebé**) | baby sling

la lavandería (^C el lavadero) · utility room

la colada · laundry

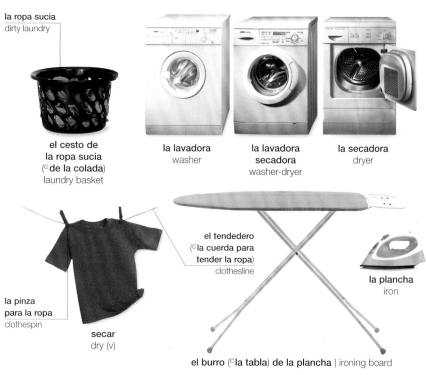

la ropa sucia
dirty laundry

el cesto de
la ropa sucia
(^C de la colada)
laundry basket

la lavadora
washer

la lavadora
secadora
washer-dryer

la secadora
dryer

el tendedero
(^C la cuerda para
tender la ropa)
clothesline

la plancha
iron

la pinza
para la ropa
clothespin

secar
dry (v)

el burro (^C la tabla) de la plancha | ironing board

---

vocabulario · vocabulary

cargar load (v)	**centrifugar** spin (v)	**planchar** iron (v)	**¿Cómo funciona la lavadora?** How do I operate the washing machine?
aclarar rinse (v)	**la centrífuga** (^C la centrifugadora) spin-dryer	**el suavizante** fabric softener	**¿Cuál es el programa para la ropa de color / blanca?** What is the setting for colors / whites?

el equipo de limpieza • cleaning equipment

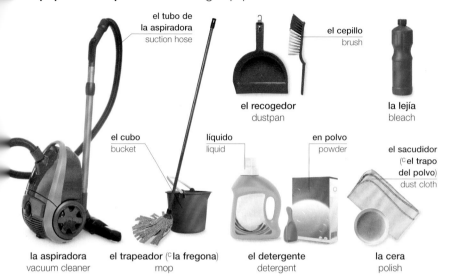

el tubo de
la aspiradora
suction hose

el cepillo
brush

el recogedor
dustpan

la lejía
bleach

el cubo
bucket

líquido
liquid

en polvo
powder

el sacudidor
(ᶜel trapo
del polvo)
dust cloth

la aspiradora
vacuum cleaner

el trapeador (ᶜla fregona)
mop

el detergente
detergent

la cera
polish

las acciones • activities

limpiar
clean (v)

fregar
wash (v)

trapear (ᶜpasar la bayeta)
wipe (v)

restregar
scrub (v)

raspar
scrape (v)

la escoba
broom

barrer
sweep (v)

sacudir (ᶜlimpiar el polvo)
dust (v)

pulir (ᶜsacar brillo)
polish (v)

el taller • workshop

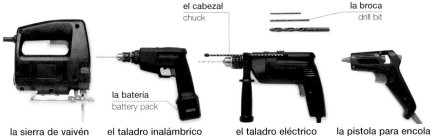

el cabezal
chuck

la broca
drill bit

la batería
battery pack

la sierra de vaivén
jigsaw

el taladro inalámbrico
cordless drill

el taladro eléctrico
electric drill

la pistola para encola
glue gun

la abrazadera
clamp

la cuchilla
blade

**el tornillo (ᶜel torno)
de banco** | vise

la lijadora
sander

la sierra circular
circular saw

el banco de trabajo
workbench

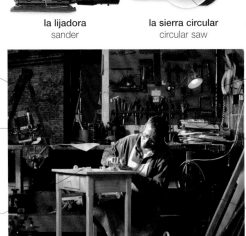

el pegamento (ᶜla
cola) de carpintero
wood glue

el organizador de
las herramientas
tool rack

la rebajadora
router

el taladro manual
bit brace

las virutas de madera
wood shavings

la extensión
(ᶜel alargador)
extension cord

...as técnicas • techniques

cortar
cut (v)

serrar
saw (v)

taladrar
drill (v)

clavar
hammer (v)

cepillar (ᶜalisar)
plane (v)

tornear
turn (v)

la soldadura
(ᶜel hilo de estaño)
solder

tallar
carve (v)

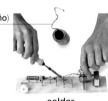
soldar
solder (v)

los materiales • materials

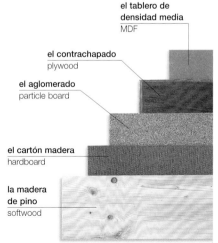

**el tablero de
densidad media**
MDF

el contrachapado
plywood

el aglomerado
particle board

el cartón madera
hardboard

**la madera
de pino**
softwood

la madera | wood

**la madera de
frondosas**
hardwood

el barniz
varnish

**el tinte para
madera**
wood stain

el alambre
wire

el cable
cable

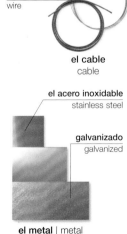
el acero inoxidable
stainless steel

galvanizado
galvanized

el metal | metal

la caja de las herramientas • toolbox

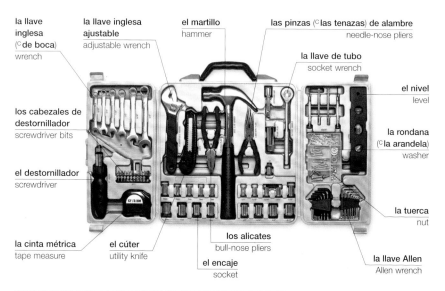

la llave inglesa (^C de boca)
wrench

la llave inglesa ajustable
adjustable wrench

el martillo
hammer

las pinzas (^C las tenazas) de alambre
needle-nose pliers

la llave de tubo
socket wrench

el nivel
level

los cabezales de destornillador
screwdriver bits

la rondana (^C la arandela)
washer

el destornillador
screwdriver

la tuerca
nut

la cinta métrica
tape measure

el cúter
utility knife

los alicates
bull-nose pliers

el encaje
socket

la llave Allen
Allen wrench

las brocas • drill bits

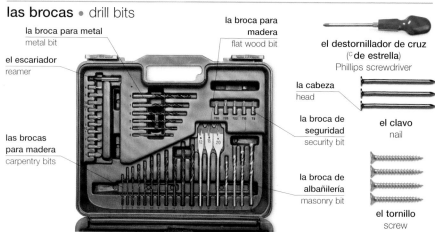

la broca para metal
metal bit

la broca para madera
flat wood bit

el escariador
reamer

el destornillador de cruz (^C de estrella)
Phillips screwdriver

la cabeza
head

la broca de seguridad
security bit

el clavo
nail

las brocas para madera
carpentry bits

la broca de albañilería
masonry bit

el tornillo
screw

el pelacables
wire strippers

el cortaalambres
wire cutters

el soldador
soldering iron

la cinta
aislante
electrical
tape

la
soldadura
solder

el escalpelo
craft knife

la sierra de calar
fretsaw

el serrucho de costilla | tenon saw

las gafas de
seguridad
safety goggles

el cepillo
plane

la caja para cortar
en inglete
miter block

el serrucho
handsaw

el taladro manual
hand drill

la lana de acero
steel wool

el papel de lija
sandpaper

la sierra para metales
hacksaw

las tenazas
wrench

el formón
chisel

la lima
file

la piedra
afiladora
whetstone

el cortatuberías | pipe cutter

el destapacaños
(ᶜel desatascador)
plunger

la decoración • decorating

las tijeras
scissors

el cúter
utility knife

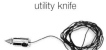

la plomada
(c la cuerda de plomada)
plumb line

la espátula (c el raspador)
putty knife

el decorador *m*
la decoradora *f*
decorator

el papel tapiz
(c el papel pintado)
wallpaper

la brocha
de tapicero
(c empapelador)
wallpaper brush

la mesa
de encolar
pasting table

la brocha
de encolar
pasting brush

el pegamento
para tapizar
(c la cola para
empapelar)
wallpaper paste

la cubeta
(c el cubo)
bucket

tapizar (c empapelar) | wallpaper (v)

despegar (c arrancar)
strip (v)

rellenar
fill (v)

lijar
sand (v)

enyesar
plaster (v)

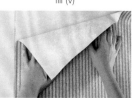

empapelar
hang (v)

poner azulejos (c alicatar)
tile (v)

el rodillo
roller

la bandeja para
la pintura
paint tray

la brocha
brush

la lata
de pintura
paint can

la escalera
de mano
stepladder

la pintura
paint

el mastique (ᶜla masilla)
filler

pintar
paint (v)

la esponja
sponge

el masking tape (ᶜla cinta
adhesiva protectora)
masking tape

el papel de lija
sandpaper

la trementina
turpentine

el aguarrás
paint thinner

vocabulario • vocabulary

el yeso plaster	mate matte	la plantilla stencil	el solvente (ᶜel disolvente) solvent	el sellador (ᶜel sellante) sealant
el barniz varnish	la base (ᶜla imprimación) primer	el papel estampado en relieve embossed paper	el conservante preservative	el protector drop cloth
la pintura de látex latex paint	el papel de apresto lining paper	la primera mano undercoat	el cemento blanco grout	el overol (ᶜel mono) coveralls
con brillo gloss		la última mano top coat		

el jardín • garden

los estilos de jardín • garden styles

los adornos para el jardín
garden features

el patio con jardín (ᶜ la terraza ajardinada)
patio garden

el jardín clásico | formal garden

el jardín campestre
cottage garden

el jardín de plantas herbáceas
herb garden

el jardín en la azotea
roof garden

la rocalla
rock garden

el patio
courtyard

el jardín acuático
water garden

la cesta colgante
hanging basket

la enredadera
(ᶜ **la espaldera**) | trellis

la pérgola
arbor

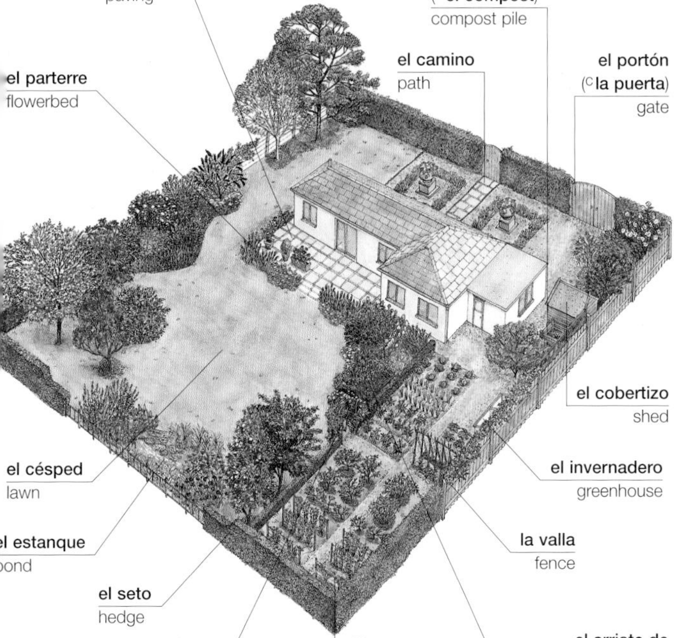

la terraza
paving

la composta
(C el compost)
compost pile

el parterre
flowerbed

el camino
path

el portón
(C la puerta)
gate

la tierra
soil

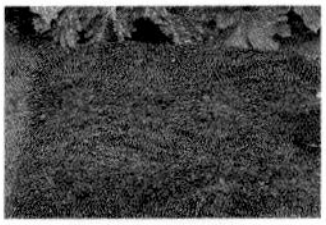

la capa superior
de la tierra
topsoil

el césped
lawn

el cobertizo
shed

la arena
sand

el estanque
pond

el invernadero
greenhouse

la valla
fence

la creta
chalk

el seto
hedge

el arco
arch

el huerto
vegetable
garden

el arriate de
plantas herbáceas
herbaceous border

el cieno
silt

el entarimado
deck

la fuente | fountain

la arcilla
clay

las plantas de jardín • garden plants

los tipos de plantas • types of plants

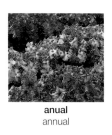
anual
annual

bienal
biennial

perenne
perennial

el bulbo
bulb

el helecho
fern

el junco
cattail

el bambú
bamboo

las malas hierbas
weeds

la hierba
herb

la planta acuática
water plant

el árbol
tree

la palmera
palm

la conífera
conifer

de hoja perenne
evergreen

de hoja caduca
deciduous

la poda ornamental
topiary

la planta alpestre
alpine

la planta suculenta
succulent

el cactus
cactus

la planta de maceta
potted plant

la planta de sombra
shade plant

la planta
trepadora
climber

el arbusto
de flor
flowering shrub

la planta para
cubrir suelo
ground cover

la planta trepadora
creeper

ornamental
ornamental

el pasto
(ᶜel césped)
grass

las herramientas de jardinería • garden tools

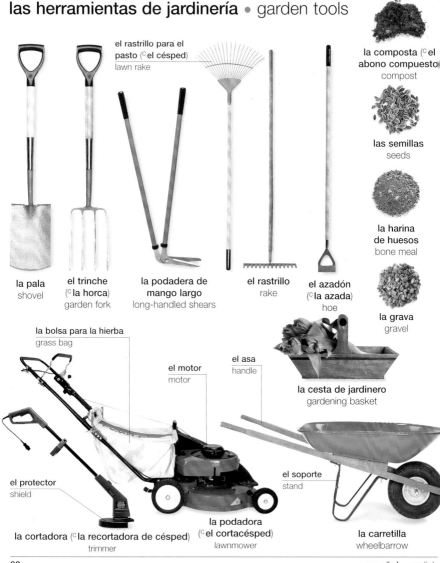

la composta (ᶜ**el abono compuesto**)
compost

las semillas
seeds

la harina de huesos
bone meal

la grava
gravel

el rastrillo para el pasto (ᶜ**el césped**)
lawn rake

la pala
shovel

el trinche (ᶜ**la horca**)
garden fork

la podadera de mango largo
long-handled shears

el rastrillo
rake

el azadón (ᶜ**la azada**)
hoe

la bolsa para la hierba
grass bag

el motor
motor

el asa
handle

la cesta de jardinero
gardening basket

el protector
shield

el soporte
stand

la cortadora (ᶜ**la recortadora de césped**)
trimmer

la podadora (ᶜ**el cortacésped**)
lawnmower

la carretilla
wheelbarrow

el trinche (^C la horquilla)
hand fork

la pala pequeña
trowel

la hoja
blade

las tijeras (^C la cizalla)
shears

el serrucho
handsaw

las podadoras
(^C las tijeras de podar)
pruners

el semillero
seed tray

el pesticida
pesticide

los guantes de jardín
gardening gloves

el hilo de
bramante
twine

las etiquetas
labels

el alambre
twist ties

las anillas
ring ties

las cañas
canes

la criba
sieve

la maceta
plant pot

las botas de goma
rubber boots

el riego • watering

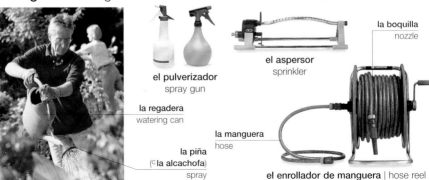

el pulverizador
spray gun

la regadera
watering can

la piña
(^C la alcachofa)
spray

el aspersor
sprinkler

la boquilla
nozzle

la manguera
hose

el enrollador de manguera | hose reel

la jardinería • gardening

el pasto
(ᶜ el césped)
lawn

el seto
hedge

el parterre
flowerbed

la podadora
(ᶜ el corta-
césped)
lawnmower

la estaca
stake

cortar el césped | mow (v)

poner césped
sod (v)

**hacer agujeros con la
trinche** (ᶜ **la horquilla**)
spike (v)

rastrillar
rake (v)

podar
trim (v)

cavar
dig (v)

sembrar
sow (v)

abonar en la superficie
top dress (v)

regar
water (v)

español • english

la caña
cane

guiar
train (v)

quitar las flores muertas
deadhead (v)

rociar
spray (v)

injertar
graft (v)

el esqueje
cutting

propagar
propagate (v)

podar
prune (v)

apuntalar
stake (v)

transplantar
transplant (v)

escardar
weed (v)

cubrir la tierra
mulch (v)

cosechar
harvest (v)

vocabulario • vocabulary

cultivar cultivate (v)	diseñar landscape (v)	abonar fertilize (v)	cribar sift (v)	el drenaje drainage	el plantón seedling	el subsuelo subsoil
cuidar tend (v)	plantar en tiesto pot (v)	coger pick (v)	airear aerate (v)	orgánico *m* **orgánica** *f* organic	el abono fertilizer	el herbicida weedkiller

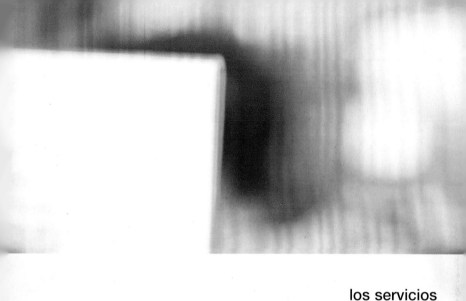

los servicios
services

los servicios de emergencia • emergency services

la ambulancia • ambulance

la camilla
stretcher

la ambulancia
ambulance

el paramédico m / **la paramédica** f
paramedic

la policía • police

la placa
badge

el uniforme
uniform

la sirena
siren

las luces
lights

la patrulla (ᶜ**el coche de policía**)
police car

la comisaría
police station

la macana
(ᶜ**la porra**)
nightstick

la pistola
gun

las esposas
handcuffs

el oficial de policía m / **la oficial de policía** f
(ᶜ**el agente de policía** m / **la agente de policía** f)
police officer

vocabulario • vocabulary

el crimen crime	**el robo** burglary	**la denuncia** complaint	**el arresto** arrest
el inspector m **la inspectora** f inspector	**la agresión** assault	**la investigación** investigation	**la celda** police cell
el detective m **la detective** f detective	**la huella** **dactilar** (ᶜ**dactilar**) fingerprint	**el sospechoso** m **la sospechosa** f suspect	**el cargo** charge

os bomberos • fire department

el casco
helmet

el humo
smoke

la manguera
hose

la cesta
basket

el chorro
de agua
water jet

los bomberos *m*
las bomberas *f*
firefighters

el brazo
boom

la escalera
ladder

la cabina
cab

el incendio | fire

la estación (ᶜel
parque) de bomberos
fire station

la escalera (ᶜla salida)
de incendios
fire escape

el camión de bomberos
fire engine

el detector
de humo
smoke alarm

la alarma contra
incendios
fire alarm

el hacha
ax

el extintor
fire extinguisher

el hidrante
hydrant

Necesito bomberos / una ambulancia. I need the police / fire department / an ambulance.	**Hay un incendio en…** There's a fire at…	**Ha habido un accidente.** There's been an accident. **¡Llame a la policía!** Call the police!

el banco • bank

la ventanilla
window

el cajero *m* la cajera *f*
teller

el cliente *m*
la clienta *f*
customer

el
mostrador
counter

la tarjeta de débito
debit card

la tarjeta de crédito
credit card

el lector de tarjetas
card reader

el número
de cuenta
account number

la cantidad
amount

las fichas de depósito
(^c las hojas de ingreso)
deposit slips

---

vocabulario • vocabulary

los ahorros savings	**la hipoteca** mortgage	**el pago** payment	**depositar** (^c**ingresar**) deposit (v)	**la cuenta corriente** checking account
el sobregiro (^c**el descubierto**) overdraft	**la tasa** (^c**el tipo**) **de interés** interest rate	**la hoja de** **reintegro** withdrawal slip	**el NIP** (^c**el pin**) PIN	**la cuenta de ahorros** savings account
el préstamo loan	**los impuestos** tax	**el débito directo** (^c**la domiciliación** **bancaria**) automatic payment	**la transferencia** **bancaria** bank transfer	**la comisión** **bancaria** bank charge

la applicación
del banco
banking app

el billete
bill

la moneda
coin

la pantalla
screen

el teclado
keypad

la ranura
de tarjeta
card reader

la banca electrónica
online banking

el dinero
money

el cajero automático
ATM

las divisas
foreign currency

la oficina de cambio
currency exchange

el tipo
de cambio
exchange rate

las finanzas • finance

el valor de las acciones
share price

el agente de bolsa m
la agente de bolsa f
stockbroker

el asesor financiero m
la asesora financiera f
financial advisor

la bolsa de valores
stock exchange

---

vocabulario • vocabulary

cobrar
cash (v)

la denominación
(ᶜ **el valor nominal**)
denomination

la comisión
commission

la inversión
investment

las acciones
shares

las acciones
stocks

el contador m
la contadora f
(ᶜ **el contable** m
la contable f)
accountant

los dividendos
dividends

la cartera
portfolio

el patrimonio neto
equity

la moneda digital
digital currency

¿Podría cambiar esto por favor?
Can I change this, please?

**¿Cómo está el tipo de
cambio hoy?**
What's today's exchange rate?

---

las comunicaciones • communications

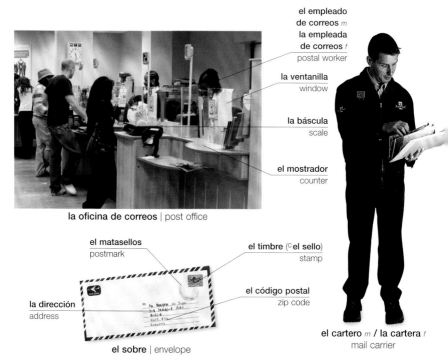

el empleado
de correos *m*
la empleada
de correos *f*
postal worker

la ventanilla
window

la báscula
scale

el mostrador
counter

la oficina de correos | post office

el matasellos
postmark

el timbre (ᶜel sello)
stamp

la dirección
address

el código postal
zip code

el sobre | envelope

el cartero *m* / la cartera *f*
mail carrier

vocabulario • vocabulary

la carta letter	**la firma** signature	**el reparto** delivery	**la bolsa de correo** (ᶜ**la saca postal**) mailbag
por avión by airmail	**la recogida** pickup	**el franqueo** postage	**no doblar** do not bend (v)
el correo certificado registered mail	**el remitente** (ᶜ**el remite**) return address	**frágil** fragile	**hacia arriba** this way up

el buzón
mailbox

el buzón
letter slot

el paquete
package

el mensajero *m*
la mensajería *f*
courier

el teléfono • telephone

el auricular
handset

la contestadora
(ᶜ **el contestador
automático**)
answering machine

la base
base station

el teclado
keypad

el teléfono inalámbrico
cordless phone

la aplicación
app

**el teléfono
inteligente**
smartphone

---

vocabulario • vocabulary

marcar
dial (v)

contestar
answer (v)

**el mensaje de texto
(SMS)**
text (SMS)

el mensaje de voz
voice message

ocupado (ᶜ **comunicando**)
busy

desconectado (ᶜ **apagado**)
disconnected

la clave de acceso
passcode

el teléfono celular
(ᶜ **el teléfono móvil**)
cell phone

**el teléfono
público**
payphone

**los datos
para celular**
mobile data

el Wi-Fi (ᶜ **la Wi-Fi**)
Wi-Fi

el roaming
data roaming

**¿Me podría dar el
número de… ?**
Can you give me the
number for… ?

**¿Cuál es el prefijo de larga
distancia para llamar a… ?**
What is the area code for… ?

**¡Mándame un mensaje
de texto!**
Text me!

el hotel • hotel

el lobby (ᶜel vestíbulo) • lobby

la tarjeta llave
key card

el huésped *m*
la huésped *f*
guest

el recepcionista *m*
la recepcionista *f*
receptionist

el mostrador
counter

la recepción | reception

el equipaje
luggage

el diablito
(ᶜel carrito)
cart

el botones *m* / la botones *f*
porter

el elevador (ᶜel ascensor)
elevator

el número de
la habitación
room number

los habitaciones • rooms

la habitación sencilla
(ᶜindividual)
single room

la habitación doble
double room

la habitación con dos
camas individuales
twin room

el baño (ᶜel cuarto
de baño) privado
private bathroom

los servicios • services

la charola (ᶜ la bandeja) del desayuno
breakfast tray

el servicio
de limpieza
maid service

el servicio
de lavandería
laundry service

el servicio de habitaciones | room service

el minibar
minibar

el restaurante
restaurant

el gimnasio
gym

la piscina
swimming pool

vocabulario • vocabulary

la pensión completa
all meals included

la media pensión
some meals included

**la habitación con
desayuno incluido**
bed and breakfast

**¿Tiene alguna habitación
libre?**
Do you have any vacancies?

**Tengo una reservación
(ᶜ reserva).**
I have a reservation.

**Quiero una habitación
sencilla (ᶜ individual).**
I'd like a single room.

**Quiero una habitación para
tres noches.**
I'd like a room for three nights.

¿Cuánto cuesta la habitación por día?
What is the charge per night?

**¿Cuándo tengo que dejar
la habitación?**
When do I have to check out?

las compras
shopping

el centro comercial • shopping center

el atrio
atrium

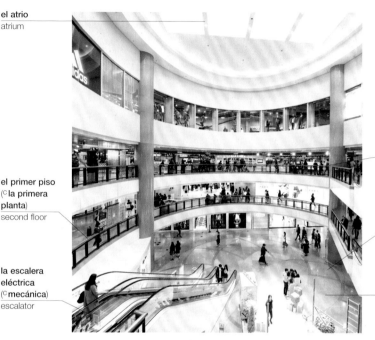

el segundo
piso (^Cla
segunda
planta)
third floor

el primer piso
(^Cla primera
planta)
second floor

la planta
baja
ground floor

la escalera
eléctrica
(^Cmecánica)
escalator

el cliente *m*
la clienta *f*
customer

---

vocabulario • vocabulary

el departamento (^Cla sección) de zapatería
shoe department

la sección de niños
children's department

el departamento (^Cla sección) de equipajes
luggage department

el servicio al cliente
customer services

el directorio
store directory

el dependiente *m*
la dependienta *f*
sales clerk

el cuarto para cambiar a los bebés
baby changing room

los probadores
fitting rooms

los baños (^Clos aseos)
restroom

¿Cuánto cuesta esto?
How much is this?

¿Puedo cambiar esto?
May I exchange this?

os grandes almacenes • department store

la ropa de caballero
menswear

la ropa de dama
(ᶜ **de señora**)
womens wear

la lencería
lingerie

la perfumería
perfumes

los cosméticos
(ᶜ **los productos de belleza**)
cosmetics

los blancos
(ᶜ **la ropa de hogar**)
linens

el mobiliario para el hogar
home furnishings

la mercería
notions

los artículos de cocina
(ᶜ **el menaje de hogar**)
kitchenware

la porcelana
china

los aparatos eléctronicos
electronics

la iluminación
lighting

los artículos deportivos
sportswear

la juguetería
toys

la papelería
stationery

los abarrotes
(ᶜ **el supermercado**)
groceries

el supermercado • supermarket

el cliente *m*
la clienta *f*
customer

el cajero *m*
la cajera *f*
cashier

el pasillo
aisle

el estante
shelf

las ofertas
specials

la caja | checkout

la bolsa de la compra
shopping bag

la caja
cash register

la banda (^Cla cinta)
transportadora
conveyor belt

la compra
groceries

el asa
handle

780863 185779

el código de barras
bar code

el carrito (^Cel carro)
grocery cart

la canasta (^Cla cesta)
basket

el escáner
scanner

la panadería
bakery

los lácteos
dairy

los cereales
breakfast cereals

las conservas
canned food

la dulcería
(ᶜ **los golosinas**)
candy

la verdura
vegetables

la fruta
fruit

**la carne y
las aves**
meat and poultry

el pescado
fish

**los comestibles
finos**
deli

los congelados
frozen food

**los platos
preparados**
prepared food

las bebidas
drinks

**los productos
de limpieza**
household products

**los artículos
de aseo**
toiletries

**los artículos
para el bebé**
baby products

**los
electrodomésticos**
electrical goods

**la comida
para animales**
pet food

las revistas | magazines

la farmacia • drugstore

la higiene femenina
feminine hygiene

el cuidado dental
dental care

los desodorantes
deodorants

las vitaminas
vitamins

el dispensari
dispensar

el farmacéutico *m*
la farmacéutica
pharmacis

el jarabe para la tos
cough medicine

los remedios
naturistas
(ᶜde herbolario)
herbal remedies

el cuidado de la piel
skin care

la crema para
después del sol
aftersun lotion

la crema protectora
sunscreen

la crema protectora
total
sun block

el repelente de insectos
insect repellent

la toallita húmeda
wet wipe

el pañuelo desechable
(ᶜde papel)
tissue

las toallas femeninas
(ᶜla compresa)
sanitary napkin

el tampón
tampon

el pantiprotector
(ᶜel salvaslip)
panty liner

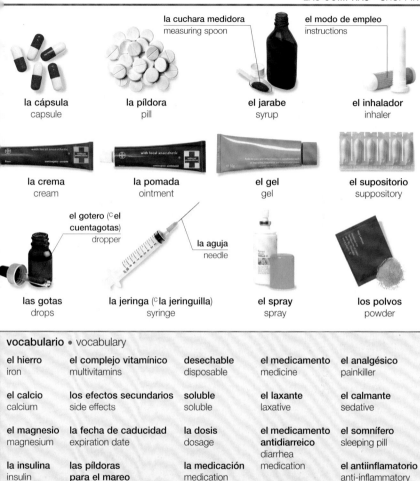

la cuchara medidora
measuring spoon

el modo de empleo
instructions

la cápsula
capsule

la píldora
pill

el jarabe
syrup

el inhalador
inhaler

la crema
cream

la pomada
ointment

el gel
gel

el supositorio
suppository

el gotero (ᶜ el
cuentagotas)
dropper

la aguja
needle

las gotas
drops

la jeringa (ᶜ la jeringuilla)
syringe

el spray
spray

los polvos
powder

vocabulario • vocabulary

el hierro iron	**el complejo vitamínico** multivitamins	**desechable** disposable	**el medicamento** medicine	**el analgésico** painkiller
el calcio calcium	**los efectos secundarios** side effects	**soluble** soluble	**el laxante** laxative	**el calmante** sedative
el magnesio magnesium	**la fecha de caducidad** expiration date	**la dosis** dosage	**el medicamento antidiarreico** diarrhea medication	**el somnífero** sleeping pill
la insulina insulin	**las píldoras para el mareo** motion-sickness pills	**la medicación** medication		**el antiinflamatorio** anti-inflammatory
		la mascarilla face mask	**la pastilla para la garganta** throat lozenge	

la florería (᠌ᶜ la floristería) • florist

las flores
flowers

la azucena
lily

la acacia
acacia

el clavel
carnation

la maceta
potted plant

la gladiol᠌
(ᶜ el gladiolo᠌
gladiolu᠌

el iri᠌
iri᠌

la margarit᠌
dais᠌

el crisantemo᠌
chrysanthemum᠌

la nube᠌
(ᶜ la gypsofila)
baby's breath᠌

el alhelí
stock

la gerbera
gerbera

el follaje
foliage

la rosa
rose

la fresia
freesia

el florero (ᶜ**el jarrón**)
vase

la orquídea
orchid

la peonía
peony

el ramo
bunch

el tallo
stem

el narciso
daffodil

el capullo
bud

la envoltura
(ᶜ**el envoltorio**)
wrapping

el tulipán | tulip

los arreglos • arrangements

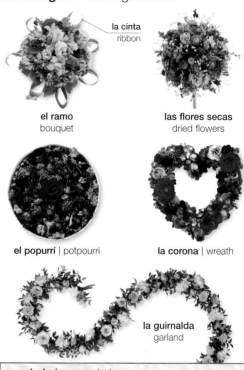

la cinta
ribbon

el ramo
bouquet

las flores secas
dried flowers

el popurrí | potpourri

la corona | wreath

la guirnalda
garland

vocabulario • vocabulary

**¿Me da un ramo de…
por favor?**
Can I have a bunch of…
please?

¿Me los puede envolver?
Can I have them wrapped?

¿Puedo poner un mensaje?
Can I attach a message?

¿Los puede enviar a… ?
Can you send them to… ?

**¿Cuánto tiempo durarán
éstos?**
How long will these last?

¿Huelen?
Are they fragrant?

el puesto de periódicos (ᶜ el quiosco de prensa)
newsstand

la cajetilla
de cigarros
(ᶜ el paquete
de tabaco)
pack of cigarettes

el encendedor
(ᶜ el mechero)
lighter

el cenicero
ashtray

los timbres
(ᶜ los sellos)
stamps

la tarjeta postal
postcard

la historieta (ᶜ el tebeo)
comic book

la revista
magazine

el periódico
newspaper

fumar • smoking

el tabaco
tobacco

el puro
cigar

**el cigarrillo
electrónico**
vape

**el líquido para
cigarrillo electrónico**
vape liquid

a dulcería (C la tienda de caramelos) • candy store

la caja de chocolates
(C de bombones)
box of chocolates

la barrita
snack bar

las papas
(C patatas) fritas
potato chips

vocabulario • vocabulary

**el chocolate
de leche
(C el chocolate
con leche)**
milk chocolate

**el chocolate
negro**
dark chocolate

**el chocolate
blanco**
white chocolate

**los dulces
(C las golosinas)
a granel**
pick and mix

el caramelo
caramel

la trufa
truffle

la galleta
cookie

los dulces (C las golosinas) • confectionery

**el chocolate
(C el bombón)**
chocolate

**la tablilla (C la tableta)
de chocolate**
chocolate bar

los caramelos
hard candy

la paleta (C la piruleta)
lollipop

el tofe
toffee

el turrón
nougat

el malvarisco (C la nube)
marshmallow

la pastilla de menta
mint

el chicle
chewing gum

las grageas
jellybean

la gomita (C la gominola)
gumdrop

el regaliz
licorice

las otras tiendas • other stores

la panadería
bakery

la confitería
pastry shop

la carnicería
butcher shop

la pescadería
fish counter

el puesto de verduras
produce stand

los abarrotes
(ᶜ**la tienda de comestible**)
grocery store

la zapatería
shoe store

la ferretería
hardware store

la tienda de antigüedades
antiques store

la tienda de regalos
(ᶜ**de artículos de regalo**)
gift shop

la agencia de viajes
travel agency

la joyería
jewelry store

la librería
bookstore

la tienda de licores
liquor store

la tienda de mascotas (^C**la pajarería**)
pet supplies store

la mueblería
(^C**la tienda de muebles**)
furniture store

la boutique
boutique

vocabulario • vocabulary

el vivero
garden center

la tintorería
dry cleaner

**la tienda
delicatessen**
(^C**la charcutería**)
delicatessen

la cerrajería
locksmith's

**la agencia
inmobiliaria**
real estate office

la lavandería
laundromat

la tienda naturista
(^C**la herboristería**)
health food store

**la tienda de
artículos usados**
second-hand store

la tienda de arte
art supply store

la sastrería
tailor shop

la estética
(^C**la peluquería**)
salon

la tienda de celulares
(^C**la tienda de móviles**)
phone store

la reparación de calzado
(^C**la zapatería**)
shoe repairs

el mercado | market

los alimentos
food

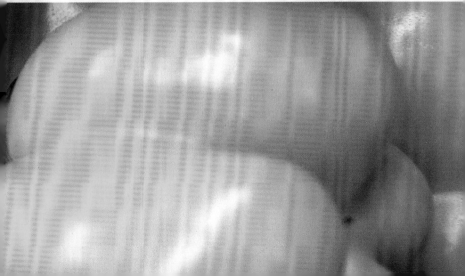

la carne • meat

el cordero
lamb

el carnicero *m*
la carnicera *f*
butcher

el gancho
meat hook

la báscula
(^C el peso)
scale

el afilador
knife sharpener

el tocino (^C el bacon)
bacon

las salchichas
sausages

el hígado
liver

---

vocabulario • vocabulary

el cerdo pork	**la cabra** goat	**la lengua** tongue	**de granja** free range	**la carne roja** red meat
la vaca beef	**el conejo** rabbit	**las asaduras** variety meat	**la carne blanca** white meat	**la carne magra** lean meat
la ternera veal	**kosher** kosher	**curado** *m* **curada** *f* cured	**orgánico** *m* **orgánica** *f* organic	**el fiambre** cooked meat
el venado venison	**halal** halal	**ahumado** *m* **ahumada** *f* smoked	**la carne de caza** game	

los cortes • cuts

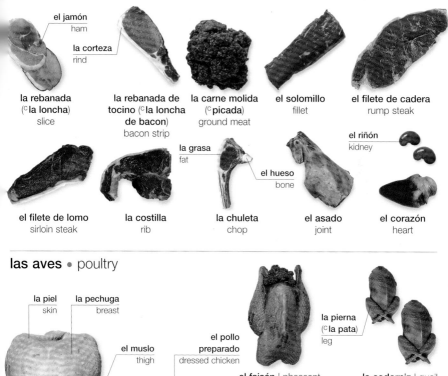

la rebanada
(ᶜ **la loncha**)
slice

el jamón
ham

la corteza
rind

la rebanada de tocino (ᶜ **la loncha de bacon**)
bacon strip

la carne molida
(ᶜ **picada**)
ground meat

el solomillo
fillet

el filete de cadera
rump steak

el filete de lomo
sirloin steak

la costilla
rib

la grasa
fat

el hueso
bone

la chuleta
chop

el asado
joint

el riñón
kidney

el corazón
heart

las aves • poultry

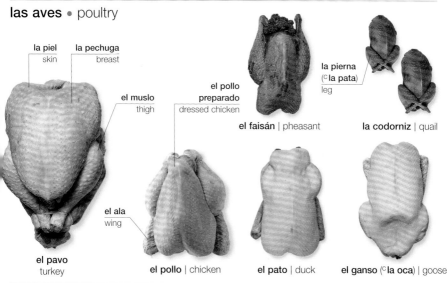

la piel
skin

la pechuga
breast

el muslo
thigh

el ala
wing

el pavo
turkey

el pollo preparado
dressed chicken

el pollo | chicken

el faisán | pheasant

la pierna
(ᶜ **la pata**)
leg

la codorniz | quail

el pato | duck

el ganso (ᶜ **la oca**) | goose

el pescado • fish

la aleta
fin

la trucha
trout

el rape
monkfish

el pez espada
swordfish

la sardina
sardine

la caballa
mackerel

el abadejo
haddock

la raya
skate

el besugo
sea bream

la cola
tail

el bacalao
cod

la lubina
sea bass

el atún
tuna

la escama
scale

el salmón | salmon

el salmonete
red mullet

la platija
lemon sole

la trucha arco iris
rainbow trout

la pescadilla
whiting

el lenguado
Dover sole

el mero
halibut

el marisco • seafood

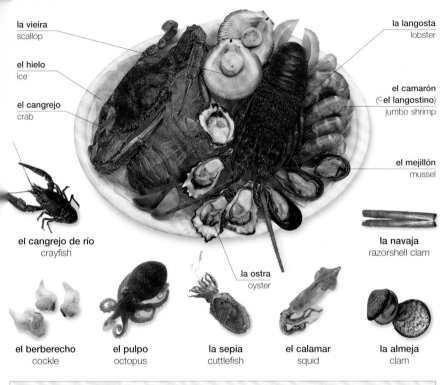

la vieira
scallop

el hielo
ice

el cangrejo
crab

la langosta
lobster

el camarón
(ᶜ el langostino)
jumbo shrimp

el mejillón
mussel

el cangrejo de río
crayfish

la navaja
razorshell clam

la ostra
oyster

el berberecho
cockle

el pulpo
octopus

la sepia
cuttlefish

el calamar
squid

la almeja
clam

vocabulario • vocabulary

congelado m congelada f frozen	limpio m limpia f cleaned	el camarón (ᶜ la gamba) shrimp	sin piel skinned	sin espinas boned	el filete fillet	el lomo loin
fresco m fresca f fresh	salado m salada f salted	ahumado m ahumada f smoked	sin escamas scaled	en filetes filleted	la rodaja steak	la espina bone

¿Me lo puede limpiar?
Will you clean it for me?

las verduras • vegetables (1)

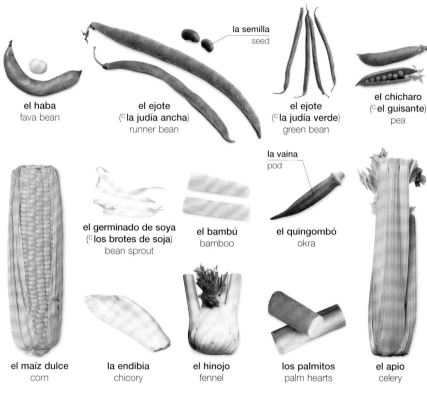

la semilla
seed

el haba
fava bean

el ejote
(ᶜla judía ancha)
runner bean

el ejote
(ᶜla judía verde)
green bean

el chícharo
(ᶜel guisante)
pea

la vaina
pod

el germinado de soya
(ᶜlos brotes de soja)
bean sprout

el bambú
bamboo

el quingombó
okra

el maíz dulce
corn

la endibia
chicory

el hinojo
fennel

los palmitos
palm hearts

el apio
celery

---

vocabulario • vocabulary

la hoja leaf	**la cabezuela** floret	**la punta** tip	**orgánico** *m* **orgánica** *f* organic	**¿Vende verduras orgánicas?** Do you sell organic vegetables?
el tallo stalk	**la almendra** kernel	**el corazón** (ᶜel centro) heart	**la bolsa de plástico** plastic bag	**¿Son productos locales?** Are these grown locally?

---

español • english

la rúgula (ᶜla rúcula)
arugula

el berro
watercress

el radicchio
radicchio

la col de bruselas
Brussels sprout

la acelga
Swiss chard

la col rizada
kale

la acedera
sorrel

la escarola
endive

el diente de león
dandelion

la espinaca
spinach

el colinabo
kohlrabi

la acelga china
bok choy

la lechuga
lettuce

el brócoli
broccoli

la col de Milán
cabbage

la berza
spring greens

las verduras • vegetables (2)

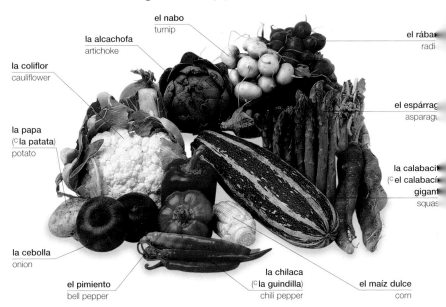

el nabo
turnip

la alcachofa
artichoke

la coliflor
cauliflower

el rábar
radi

el espárrac
asparagu

la papa
(^C la patata)
potato

la calabaci
(^C el calabací
gigant
squas

la cebolla
onion

la chilaca
(^C la guindilla)
chili pepper

el pimiento
bell pepper

el maíz dulce
corn

vocabulario • vocabulary

la mandioca cassava	**el apio-nabo** celeriac	**congelado** *m* **congelada** *f* frozen	**amargo** *m* **amarga** *f* bitter	**¿Me da un kilo de papas, por favor?** A kilo of potatoes, please.
la zanahoria carrot	**la raíz del taro** taro root	**crudo** *m* **cruda** *f* raw	**firme** *m/f* firm	**¿Cuánto vale el kilo?** What's the price per kilo?
el fruto del pan breadfruit	**la castaña de agua** water chestnut	**picante** *m/f* hot (spicy)	**la pulpa** flesh	**¿Cómo se llaman esos?** What are those called?
la papa (^C **la patata) nueva** new potato	**el jitomate** (^C **el tomate) cherry** cherry tomato	**dulce** *m/f* sweet	**la raíz** root	

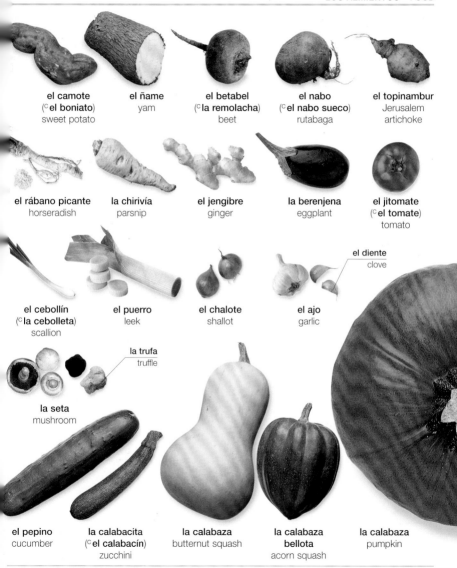

el camote
(ᶜ **el boniato**)
sweet potato

el ñame
yam

el betabel
(ᶜ **la remolacha**)
beet

el nabo
(ᶜ **el nabo sueco**)
rutabaga

el topinambur
Jerusalem
artichoke

el rábano picante
horseradish

la chirivía
parsnip

el jengibre
ginger

la berenjena
eggplant

el jitomate
(ᶜ **el tomate**)
tomato

el cebollín
(ᶜ **la cebolleta**)
scallion

el puerro
leek

el chalote
shallot

el ajo
garlic

el diente
clove

la trufa
truffle

la seta
mushroom

el pepino
cucumber

la calabacita
(ᶜ **el calabacín**)
zucchini

la calabaza
butternut squash

**la calabaza
bellota**
acorn squash

la calabaza
pumpkin

la fruta • fruit (1)

los cítricos • citrus fruit

la naranja
orange

la mandarina clementina
clementine

el ugli
ugli fruit

la piel (ᶜla médula)
pith

la toronja (ᶜel pomelo)
grapefruit

la mandarina
tangerine

el gajo
segment

la mandarina satsuma
satsuma

la cáscara
zest

la lima
lime

el limón
lemon

la naranja china (ᶜel kumquat)
kumquat

la fruta con hueso • stone fruit

el durazno
(ᶜel melocotón)
peach

la nectarina
nectarine

el chabacano
(ᶜel albaricoque)
apricot

la ciruela
plum

la cereza
cherry

la pera
pear

la manzana
apple

el frutero (ᶜla cesta de fruta) | basket of fruit

...s bayas y los melones • berries and melons

la fresa
strawberry

la frambuesa
raspberry

el melón
melon

la uva
grapes

...a zarzamora (ᶜ**la mora**)
blackberry

la grosella
red currant

la cáscara
(ᶜ**la corteza**)
rind

el arándano rojo
cranberry

la grosella negra
black currant

la semilla
(ᶜ**la pepita**)
seed

el arándano
blueberry

la grosella blanca
white currant

la pulpa
flesh

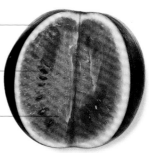

la sandía
watermelon

la frambuesa Logan
loganberry

el capulín
(ᶜ**la grosella espinosa**)
gooseberry

vocabulario • vocabulary

el ruibarbo rhubarb	**fresco** *m* **fresca** *f* fresh	**podrido** *m* **podrida** *f* rotten	**la pulpa** pulp	**¿Están maduros?** Are they ripe?
la fibra fiber	**jugoso** *m* **jugosa** *f* juicy	**el jugo** (ᶜ**el zumo**) juice	**sin semillas** (ᶜ**pepitas**) seedless	**¿Puedo probar uno?** Can I try one?
dulce *m/f* sweet				**¿Hasta cuándo durarán?** How long will they keep?
agrio *m* **agria** *f* sour	**fresco** *m* **fresca** *f* crisp	**el corazón** core		

la fruta • fruit (2)

el mango
mango

el aguacate
avocado

la piña
pineapple

la papaya
papaya

el melocotón
peach

el lichi
lychee

el capulín
(ᶜel alquequenje)
Cape gooseberry

el kiwi
kiwifruit

la semilla
seed

la piel
peel

el membrillo
quince

el maracuyá
passion fruit

el plátano
banana

la guayaba
guava

la granada
pomegranate

el caqui
persimmon

la feijoa
feijoa

la tuna
(ᶜel higo chumbo)
prickly pear

la carambola
star fruit

el tamarillo
tamarillo

os frutos seco • nuts and dried fruit

el piñón
pine nut

el pistache
(ᶜ **el pistacho**)
pistachio

la nuez de la India
(ᶜ **el anacardo**)
cashew

el cacahuate
(ᶜ **el cacahuete**)
peanut

la avellana
hazelnut

la nuez de Brasil
Brazil nut

la nuez
(ᶜ **la pacana**)
pecan

la almendra
almond

la nuez de Castilla
(ᶜ **la nuez**) | walnut

la castaña
chestnut

la macadamia
macadamia

el higo
fig

el dátil
date

la ciruela pasa
prune

la cáscara
shell

la pasa sultana
sultana

la pasa
raisin

la pasa de Corinto
currant

la pulpa
flesh

el coco
coconut

vocabulario • vocabulary

verde *m/f* green	**duro** *m* **dura** *f* hard	**la almendra** kernel	**salado** *m* **salada** *f* salted	**tostado** *m* **toastada** *f* roasted	**pelado** *m* **pelada** *f* shelled	**las frutas tropicales** tropical fruit
maduro *m* **madura** *f* ripe	**blando** *m* **blanda** *f* soft	**desecado** *m* **desecada** *f* desiccated	**crudo** *m* **cruda** *f* raw	**de temporada** seasonal	**entero** *m* **entera** *f* whole	**la fruta escarchada** candied fruit **la yaca** jackfruit

los granos y las legumbres • grains and legumes

los granos • grains

el trigo
wheat

la avena
oats

la cebada
barley

el mijo
millet

el maíz
corn

la quinoa
quinoa

vocabulario • vocabulary

la semilla seed	**fresco** m **fresca** f fresh	integral whole-grain
la cáscara husk	**perfumado** m **perfumada** f fragranced	largo long-grain
el grano kernel	**los cereales** cereal	corto short-grain
seco m **seca** f dry	**poner a remojo** soak (v)	de fácil cocción quick cooking

el arroz • rice

el arroz largo
white rice

el arroz integral
brown rice

el arroz salvaje
wild rice

el arroz bomba
arborio rice

los granos procesados
processed grains

el cuscús
couscous

el trigo partido
cracked wheat

la sémola
semolina

el salvado
bran

os frijoles y los chícharos (ᶜlas legumbres) • legumes

el frijol blanco
(ᶜla alubia blanca)
butter beans

el frijol blanco chico
(ᶜla alubia blanca
pequeña) | haricot beans

el frijol rojo
(ᶜla alubia roja)
red kidney beans

el frijol morado
(ᶜla alubia morada)
adzuki beans

los habas
fava beans

la semilla de soja
soybeans

el frijol (ᶜla alubia)
de ojo negro
black-eyed peas

el frijol pinto
(ᶜla alubia pinta)
pinto beans

el frijol mung
(ᶜla alubia mung)
mung beans

el frijol flageolet
(ᶜla alubia flageolet)
flageolet beans

la lenteja
castellana
brown lentils

la lenteja roja
red lentils

los chícharos
(ᶜlos guisantes tiernos)
green peas

los garbanzos
chickpeas

los chícharos secos
(ᶜlos guisantes secos)
split peas

las semillas • seeds

la pepita
(ᶜla pipa)
de calabaza
pumpkin seed

la semilla de
mostaza (ᶜla
mostaza en grano)
mustard seed

la semilla de alcaravea
caraway seed

la semilla de girasol
(ᶜla pipa de girasol)
sunflower seed

la semilla
de sésamo
sesame seed

las hierbas y las especias • herbs and spices

las especias • spices

la vainilla
vanilla

la nuez moscada
nutmeg

la macis
mace

la cúrcuma
turmeric

el comino
cumin

el ramillete aromático
bouquet garni

la pimienta de Jamaica
allspice

la pimienta en grano
peppercorn

el heno griego
fenugreek

el chile en polvo
chili powder

entero *m*
entera *f*
whole

machacado *m*
machacada *f*
crushed

el azafrán
saffron

el cardamomo
cardamom

el curry en polvo
curry powder

molido
ground

el pimentón
paprika

las hojuelas
(ᶜ**laminado**)
flakes

el ajo
garlic

las hierbas • herbs

las rajas
(ᶜlas ramas)
sticks

la canela
cinnamon

la citronela
lemongrass

los clavos
cloves

**el anís
estrellado**
star anise

el jengibre
ginger

el hinojo
fennel

las semillas
de hinojo
fennel seeds

el laurel
bay leaf

el perejil
parsley

el cebollino
chives

la menta
mint

el tomillo
thyme

la salvia
sage

el estragón
tarragon

la mejorana
marjoram

la albahaca
basil

el orégano
oregano

el cilantro
cilantro

el eneldo
dill

el romero
rosemary

los alimentos embotellados
bottled foods

el aceite de nueces
walnut oil

el aceite de almendras
almond oil

el aceite de semillas de uva
grapeseed oil

el corcho
cork

el aceite de girasol
sunflower oil

el aceite de sésamo
sesame seed oil

el aceite de avellanas
hazelnut oil

los aceites
oils

el aceite de oliva
olive oil

las hierbas
herbs

el aceite aromatizado
flavored oil

las conservas dulces • sweet spreads

el tarro
jar

el panal
honeycomb

la miel cristalizada
(^Ccompacta)
raw honey

la crema de limón
lemon curd

la mermelada de frambuesa
raspberry jam

la mermelada de naranja
marmalade

la miel líquida
clear honey

la miel de maple
(^Cel jarabe de arce)
maple syrup

as salsas y los condimentos
sauces and condiments

el vinagre de sidra
cider vinegar

la mayonesa
mayonnaise

el chutney
chutney

el vinagre
balsámico
balsamic vinegar

la botella
bottle

el vinagre de malta
malt vinegar

el vinagre de vino
wine vinegar

el vinagre
vinegar

la catsup
(ᶜ **el kétchup**)
ketchup

la salsa
sauce

**la mostaza
inglesa**
English mustard

**la mostaza
francesa**
Dijon mustard

**la mostaza en
grano**
whole-grain
mustard

a **crema de cacahuate**
(ᶜ **la mantequilla de
cacahuetes**)
peanut butter

el tarro hermético
canning jar

**el chocolate
para untar**
chocolate spread

**la fruta en
conserva**
preserved fruit

vocabulario • vocabulary

el aceite vegetal vegetable oil	**el aceite de colza** canola oil
el aceite de maíz corn oil	**la salsa de soya** soy sauce
el aceite de cacahuate (ᶜ **cacahuete**) peanut oil	**el aceite de presión en frío** cold-pressed oil

los productos lácteos • dairy products

el queso • cheese

la corteza
rind

el queso semicurado
semi-hard cheese

el queso rallado
grated cheese

el queso curado
hard cheese

el queso
cremoso semicurado
semi-soft cheese

el requesón
cottage cheese

el queso cremoso
cream cheese

el queso azul
blue cheese

el queso cremoso
soft cheese

el queso fresco | fresh cheese

la leche • milk

la leche
entera
whole milk

la leche
semidescremada
(ᶜ semidesnatada)
reduced-fat milk

la leche
descremada
(ᶜ desnatada)
skim milk

el cartón
de leche
milk carton

la leche
de cabra
goat's milk

la leche
condensada
condensed milk

la leche de vaca | cow's milk

la mantequilla
butter

la margarina
margarine

la crema (ᶜ**la nata**)
cream

la crema (ᶜ**la nata**) **líquida**
half-and-half

a crema para batir
la nata para montar)
heavy cream

la crema batida
(ᶜ**la nata montada**)
whipped cream

la crema ácida
(ᶜ**la nata agria**)
sour cream

el yogur
yogurt

el helado
ice cream

los huevos • eggs

la yema
egg yolk

la clara
egg white

la cáscara
shell

el huevo de gallina
hen's egg

el huevo de pato
duck egg

la huevera
eggcup

el huevo tibio
(ᶜ**pasado por agua**)
soft-boiled egg

el huevo de ganso
(ᶜ**de oca**)
goose egg

**el huevo de
codorniz**
quail egg

---

vocabulario • vocabulary

pasteurizado pasteurized	**sin grasa** fat-free	**salado** *m* **salada** *f* salted	**la leche de almendra** almond milk	**el suero de la leche** buttermilk	**la lactosa** lactose
sin pasteurizar unpasteurized	**la leche en polvo** powdered milk	**sin sal** unsalted	**la leche de avena** oat milk	**la malteada** (ᶜ**el batido**) milk shake	**el yogur helado** frozen yogurt

el pan y las harinas • breads and flours

la hogaza | loaf

la baguette | baguette

la ciabatta | ciabatta

el pan de centeno | rye bread

el croissant | croissant

la panadería | bakery

hacer pan • making bread

la harina blanca
white flour

la harina morena
brown flour

la harina integral
whole-wheat flour

**la levadura
de panadería**
yeast

cernir (ᶜ**cribar**) | sift (v)

la masa | dough

mezclar | mix (v)

amasar | knead (v)

hornear | bake (v)

la corteza
crust

el pan blanco
white bread

el pan integral
(ᶜ**moreno**)
brown bread

el pan integral
whole-wheat bread

la rebanada
slice

el pan con grano
multigrain bread

el pan de maíz
corn bread

**el pan al bicarbonato
sódico**
soda bread

el pan fermentado
sourdough bread

el pan sin levadura
flat bread

el bagel
bagel

el bollo
bun

el panecillo
roll

el pan de frutas
(ᶜ**el plumcake**)
fruit bread

el pan con semillas
seeded bread

el naan
naan bread

el pan de pita
pita bread

el pan danés
(ᶜ**el pan tostado**)
crispbread

---

vocabulario • vocabulary

la harina con levadura self-rising flour	**la harina blanca** all-purpose flour	**levar** prove (v)	**la barra** flute	**el rebanador** slicer
la harina para pan bread flour	**subir** rise (v)	**sin glúten** gluten-free	**el pan molido** (ᶜ**rallado**) breadcrumbs	**el panadero** *m* **la panadera** *f* baker

la repostería • cakes and desserts

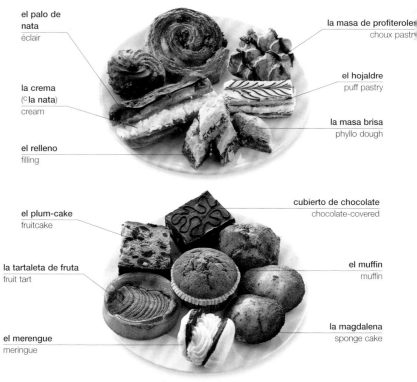

el palo de nata
éclair

la masa de profiteroles
choux pastry

el hojaldre
puff pastry

la crema
(ᶜla nata)
cream

la masa brisa
phyllo dough

el relleno
filling

el plum-cake
fruitcake

cubierto de chocolate
chocolate-covered

la tartaleta de fruta
fruit tart

el muffin
muffin

el merengue
meringue

la magdalena
sponge cake

los pasteles | cakes

---

vocabulario • vocabulary

la crema pastelera crème pâtissière	**el bollo** bun	**la masa** pastry	**la celebración** celebration	**¿Puedo tomar una rebanada (ᶜun trozo)?** May I have a slice, please?
el pastel de chocolate chocolate cake	**las natillas** custard	**la rebanada** (ᶜel trozo) slice	**el arroz con leche** rice pudding	

---

español • english

os chips (ᶜel trocito) de chocolate
chocolate chip

las soletillas
ladyfinger

la florentina
Florentine

el postre de soletillas, gelatina de frutas y crema (ᶜnata)
trifle

las galletas | cookies

el mousse (ᶜla mousse)
mousse

el sorbete
sherbet

el pastel de crema (ᶜnata)
cream pie

el flan
crème caramel

los pasteles para celebraciones (ᶜ las tartas para celebraciones) • celebration cakes

el último piso
top tier

el primer piso
bottom tier

el mazapán
marzipan

el listón (ᶜla cinta)
ribbon

el betún (ᶜla alcorza)
frosting

el pastel de bodas (ᶜla tarta nupcial) | wedding cake

la decoración
decoration

las velas de cumpleaños
birthday candles

apagar
blow out (v)

el pastel (ᶜla tarta) de cumpleaños | birthday cake

la charcutería • delicatessen

la salchicha
picante
spicy sausage

el aceite
oil

el vinagre
vinegar

la quiche
quiche

la carne fresca
uncooked meat

el mostrador
counter

el salami
salami

el salchichón
pepperoni

el paté
pâté

la mozzarella
mozzarella

el brie
Brie

el queso de cabra
goat cheese

el cheddar
cheddar

el parmesano
Parmesan

el camembert
Camembert

la corteza
rind

el queso de bola
Edam

el manchego
Manchego

los pasteles de carne
meat pies

la aceituna negra
black olive

el chile piquín
(ᶜla guindilla)
chili pepper

la salsa
sauce

el panecillo
bread roll

el fiambre
cooked meat

la aceituna verde
green olive

el jamón
ham

el mostrador de bocadillos
sandwich counter

el pescado ahumado
smoked fish

las alcaparras
capers

vocabulario • vocabulary

en aceite	salado m	ahumado m
in oil	salada f	ahumada f
	salted	smoked
en salmuera		
in brine	marinado m	curado m
	marinada f	curada f
	marinated	cured

Tome un número, por favor.
Take a number, please.

¿Puedo probar un poco de eso?
Can I try some of that, please?

¿Me pone seis rebanadas (ᶜlonchas)
de aquel?
May I have six slices of that, please?

el jamón curado
prosciutto

el chorizo
chorizo

la aceituna rellena
stuffed olive

las bebidas • drinks

el agua • water

el agua embotellada
bottled water

con gas
sparkling

sin gas
still

el agua mineral
mineral water

el agua de la llave
(ᶜ del grifo)
tap water

el agua tónica
(ᶜ la tónica)
tonic water

la soda
soda water

las bebidas calientes
hot drinks

la bolsita de té
teabag

el té en hoja
loose-leaf tea

el té
tea

los granos
beans

el café molido
ground coffee

el café
coffee

el chocolate
caliente
hot chocolate

la bebida
malteada
malted milk

los refrescos • soft drinks

el popote
(ᶜ la pajita)
straw

el jugo de jitomate
(ᶜ el zumo de tomate)
tomato juice

el jugo de frutas
(ᶜ el zumo de frutas)
fruit juice

la limonada
lemonade

la naranjada
orangeade

la cola
cola

as bebidas alcohólicas • alcoholic drinks

la ginebra
gin

la lata
can

la cerveza
beer

la sidra
hard cider

la cerveza amarga
amber ale

la cerveza negra
stout

el vodka
vodka

el whisky
whiskey

el ron
rum

el brandy (ᶜ**el coñac**)
brandy

el oporto
port

seco
dry

el vino de jerez
sherry

el sake
sake

rosado
rosé

blanco
white

tinto
red

el vino
wine

el licor
liqueur

el tequila
tequila

el champán
champagne

comer fuera
eating out

la cafetería • café

la sombril..
umbrel..

el toldo
awning

la carta
menu

la terraza
patio café

la máquina de café
coffee machine

la mes..
table

la cafetería con mesas fuera | sidewalk café

el bar | snack bar

el café • coffee

el café con leche
coffee with milk

el café solo
black coffee

la cocoa (Cel
cacao en polvo)
cocoa powder

la espuma
froth

el café de cafetera eléctrica
filter coffee

el expreso (Cel café solo)
espresso

el cappuccino
cappuccino

el café con hielo
iced coffee

el té • tea

la manzanilla
chamomile tea

el té verde
green tea

el té de hierbas
(ᶜ **la infusión**)
herbal tea

el té con leche
tea with milk

el té negro
black tea

el té con limón
tea with lemon

la menta poleo
mint tea

el té con hielo
iced tea

los jugos y las malteadas (ᶜ los zumos y los batidos) • juices and milkshakes

la malteada de chocolate
(ᶜ **el batido de chocolate**)
chocolate milkshake

la malteada de fresa (ᶜ **el batido de fresa**)
strawberry milkshake

el jugo de naranja
orange juice

el jugo de manzana (ᶜ **el zumo de manzana**)
apple juice

el jugo de piña
pineapple juice

el jugo de jitomate (ᶜ **el zumo de tomate**)
tomato juice

la malteada de café (ᶜ **el batido de café**)
coffee milkshake

la comida • food

el pan integral
whole-wheat bread

la bola
scoop

el sándwich tostado
toasted sandwich

la ensalada
salad

el helado
ice cream

el pan dulce (ᶜ **el pastel**)
pastry

el bar • bar

la cafetera (^C la máquina del café)
coffee machine

la cerveza de barril (^C el grifo de cerveza)
beer tap

el barman *m*
la barman *f*
bartender

la caja
cash register

la barra
bar counter

el posavasos
coaster

vocabulario
vocabulary

el meditor óptico
dispenser

la hielera
(^C la champanera)
ice bucket

el cenicero
ashtray

el banco
(^C el taburete)
bar stool

el destapador
(^C el abrebotellas)
bottle opener

la palanca
lever

el agitador
stirrer

las pinzas
tongs

el medidor
measure

el sacacorchos | corkscrew

la coctelera | cocktail shaker

el gin tonic
gin and tonic

la jarra
pitcher

**el whiskey escocés
con agua**
scotch and water

el cubito de hielo
ice cube

el cuba libre
rum and cola

el desarmador
(ᶜ **el vodka con naranja**)
screwdriver

el martini
martini

el cóctel
cocktail

el vino
wine

la cerveza
beer

doble
double

sencillo
single

con hielo y limón
ice and lemon

un chupito
shot

la medida
measure

sin hielo
without ice

con hielo
with ice

la botana (ᶜ **los aperitivos**) • bar snacks

las nueces de la India
(ᶜ **los anacardos**)
cashews

los cacahuates
peanuts

las almendras
almonds

las papas (ᶜ **las patatas**) **fritas**
potato chips

los frutos secos | nuts

las aceitunas | olives

el restaurante • restaurant

el cubierto
table setting

el ayudante
del chef *m*
la ayudante
del chef *f*
sous chef

la copa
glass

el chef *m*
la chef *f*
chef

la charola
(c la bandeja)
tray

la cocina
kitchen

el mesero *m* / la mesera *f*
server

vocabulario • vocabulary

la lista de vinos wine list	a la carta à la carte	el precio price	la propina tip	el bufet buffet	el cliente *m* la clienta *f* customer
el menú de la comida lunch menu	el carrito de los postres dessert cart	la cuenta check	servicio incluido service charge included	el bar bar	la pimienta pepper
el menú de la cena dinner menu	los platillos (c los platos) del día specials	el recibo receipt	servicio no incluido service charge not included	la sal salt	

la carta
menu

el menú para niños
child's meal

ordenar (ᶜ **pedir**)
order (v)

pagar
pay (v)

los platos • courses

el aperitivo
apéritif

la entrada
(ᶜ **el entrante**)
appetizer

la sopa
soup

el plato principal
entrée

el acompañamiento
side dish

el postre | dessert

el café | coffee

vocabulario • vocabulary

Una mesa para dos, por favor.
A table for two, please.

¿Podría ver la carta / lista de vinos, por favor?
Can I see the menu / wine list, please?

¿Hay menú del día?
Is there a fixed-price menu?

¿Tiene platos vegetarianos?
Do you have any vegetarian dishes?

¿Me podría traer la cuenta / un recibo?
Could I have the check / a receipt, please?

¿Podemos pagar por separado?
Can we pay separately?

¿Dónde están los baños (ᶜ los servicios), por favor?
Where is the restroom, please?

la comida rápida • fast food

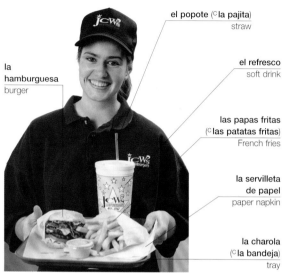

el popote (ᶜla pajita)
straw

el refresco
soft drink

la hamburguesa
burger

las papas fritas
(ᶜlas patatas fritas)
French fries

la servilleta de papel
paper napkin

la charola
(ᶜla bandeja)
tray

la hamburguesa con papas fritas
(ᶜla hamburguesa con patatas fritas) | burger meal

la entrega a domicilio
home delivery

el refresco en lata
(ᶜla lata de bebida)
canned drink

la lista de precios
price list

el puesto callejero
street vendor

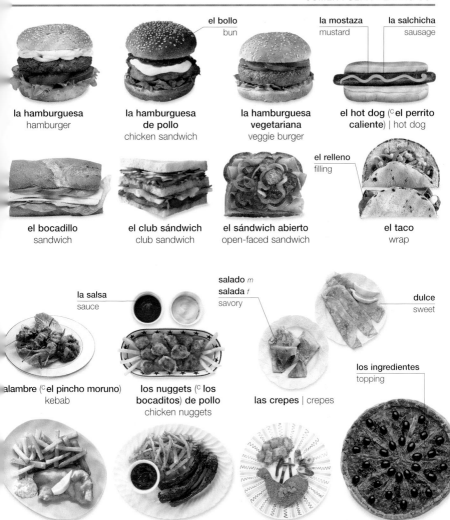

la hamburguesa
hamburger

la hamburguesa
de pollo
chicken sandwich

el bollo
bun

la hamburguesa
vegetariana
veggie burger

la mostaza
mustard

la salchicha
sausage

el hot dog (ᶜ el perrito
caliente) | hot dog

el bocadillo
sandwich

el club sándwich
club sandwich

el sándwich abierto
open-faced sandwich

el relleno
filling

el taco
wrap

la salsa
sauce

salado m
salada f
savory

dulce
sweet

los ingredientes
topping

alambre (ᶜ el pincho moruno)
kebab

los nuggets (ᶜ los
bocaditos) de pollo
chicken nuggets

las crepes | crepes

el pescado con papas fritas
(el pescado y las patatas fritas)
fish and chips

las costillas
ribs

el pollo frito
fried chicken

la pizza
pizza

el desayuno • breakfast

la leche
milk

los
cereales
cereal

la mermelada
jam

la fruta seca
(ᶜdesecada)
dried fruit

el jamón
ham

el queso
cheese

la galleta de
centeno
crispbread

el buffet de desayuno
breakfast buffet

la mermelada de naranja
marmalade

el paté
pâté

la mantequilla
butter

el jugo (ᶜel zumo)
de frutas
fruit juice

el café
coffee

el chocolate caliente
(ᶜel cacao)
hot chocolate

el croissant
croissant

el té
tea

la mesa del desayuno | breakfast table

las bebidas | drinks

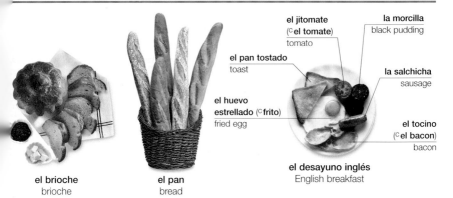

el jitomate
(ᶜel tomate)
tomato

la morcilla
black pudding

el pan tostado
toast

la salchicha
sausage

el huevo
estrellado (ᶜfrito)
fried egg

el tocino
(ᶜel bacon)
bacon

el desayuno inglés
English breakfast

el brioche
brioche

el pan
bread

la yema
egg yolk

la clara
egg white

**los arenques
ahumados**
kippers

el pan francés
(ᶜla torrija)
French toast

el huevo tibio
(ᶜpasado por agua)
soft-boiled egg

los huevos revueltos
scrambled eggs

la crema (ᶜla nata)
whipped cream

el yogur de frutas
fruit yogurt

las crepas
(ᶜlos crepes)
crepes

los waffles (ᶜlos gofres)
waffles

la avena (ᶜlas
gachas de avena)
oatmeal

la fruta fresca
fresh fruit

la comida principal • dinner

la sopa | soup

el caldo | broth

el guiso | stew

el curry | curry

el asado
roast

la empanada (ᶜel pastel)
potpie

el soufflé
soufflé

la brocheta (ᶜel pincho)
kebab

los fideos
noodles

las albóndigas
meatballs

el omelette (ᶜla tortilla)
omelet

el revuelto
stir-fry

los palillos chinos
chopsticks

la pasta | pasta

el arroz
rice

la ensalada mixta
tossed salad

la ensalada verde
green salad

el aderezo (ᶜel aliño)
dressing

as técnicas • techniques

relleno m / **rellena** f
stuffed

en salsa | in sauce

a la plancha | grilled

marinado m / **marinada** f
marinated

escalfado m
escalfada f
poached

machacado m
machacada f
mashed

horneado m
horneada f
baked

frito con poco aceite m
frita con poco aceite f
pan-fried

frito m / **frita** f
fried

en vinagre
pickled

ahumado m / **ahumada** f
smoked

frito con mucho aceite m
frita con mucho faceite f
deep-fried

en almíbar
in syrup

aderezado m / **aderezada** f
dressed

al vapor
steamed

curado m / **curada** f
cured

el estudio
study

el colegio • school

el pizarrón blanco
(ᶜ**la pizarra blanca**)
whiteboard

el maestro *m*
la maestra *f*
teacher

la mochila
(ᶜ**la cartera**)
school backpack

el alumno *m*
la alumna *f*
student

el escritorio
desk

el aula | classroom

el alumno *m* / **la alumna** *f*
student

---

vocabulario • vocabulary

la historia history	**el arte** art	**la física** physics
la literatura literature	**la música** music	**la química** chemistry
los idiomas languages	**las ciencias** science	**la biología** biology
la geografía geography	**las matemáticas** math	**la educación física** physical education

las actividades • activities

leer | read (v)

escribir | write (v)

deletrear
spell (v)

dibujar
draw (v)

la punta
nib

el color
(ᶜel lápiz de colores)
colored pencil

el
sacapuntas
pencil
sharpener

el proyector digital
digital projector

la pluma
(ᶜel bolígrafo)
pen

el lápiz
pencil

la goma
eraser

el cuaderno
notebook

el libro de texto | textbook

el estuche
pencil case

la regla
ruler

preguntar
question (v)

contestar
answer (v)

discutir
discuss (v)

aprender
learn (v)

vocabulario • vocabulary

el director *m*	**la tarea**	**la enciclopedia**
la directora *f*	(ᶜlos deberes)	encyclopedia
principal	homework	
la lección	**la redacción**	**el año**
lesson	essay	(ᶜel curso)
		year
la pregunta	**el examen**	
question	test	
la respuesta	**el diccionario**	
answer	dictionary	
tomar	**la calificación**	
apuntes	(ᶜla nota)	
take notes (v)	grade	

las matemáticas • math

las formas • shapes

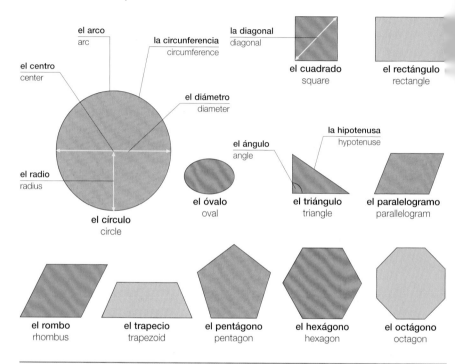

el arco
arc

la circunferencia
circumference

el centro
center

la diagonal
diagonal

el diámetro
diameter

el cuadrado
square

el rectángulo
rectangle

el radio
radius

el círculo
circle

el ángulo
angle

la hipotenusa
hypotenuse

el óvalo
oval

el triángulo
triangle

el paralelogramo
parallelogram

el rombo
rhombus

el trapecio
trapezoid

el pentágono
pentagon

el hexágono
hexagon

el octágono
octagon

los cuerpos geométricos • solids

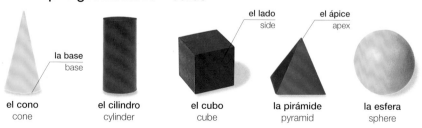

la base
base

el lado
side

el ápice
apex

el cono
cone

el cilindro
cylinder

el cubo
cube

la pirámide
pyramid

la esfera
sphere

as líneas • lines

recta
straight

paralela
parallel

perpendicular
perpendicular

curva
curved

as medidas • measurements

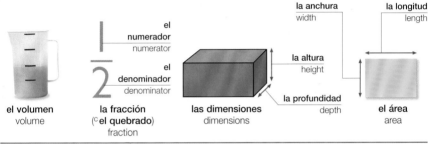

el volumen
volume

el **numerador**
numerator

el **denominador**
denominator

la fracción
(ᶜ **el quebrado**)
fraction

las dimensiones
dimensions

la anchura
width

la altura
height

la profundidad
depth

la longitud
length

el área
area

los materiales • equipment

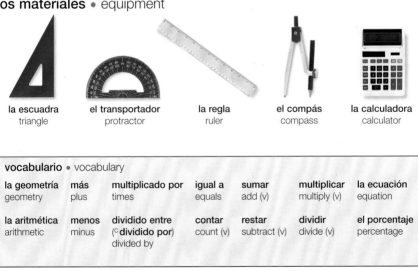

la escuadra
triangle

el transportador
protractor

la regla
ruler

el compás
compass

la calculadora
calculator

---

vocabulario • vocabulary

la geometría geometry	**más** plus	**multiplicado por** times	**igual a** equals	**sumar** add (v)	**multiplicar** multiply (v)	**la ecuación** equation
la aritmética arithmetic	**menos** minus	**dividido entre** (ᶜ **dividido por**) divided by	**contar** count (v)	**restar** subtract (v)	**dividir** divide (v)	**el porcentaje** percentage

---

las ciencias • science

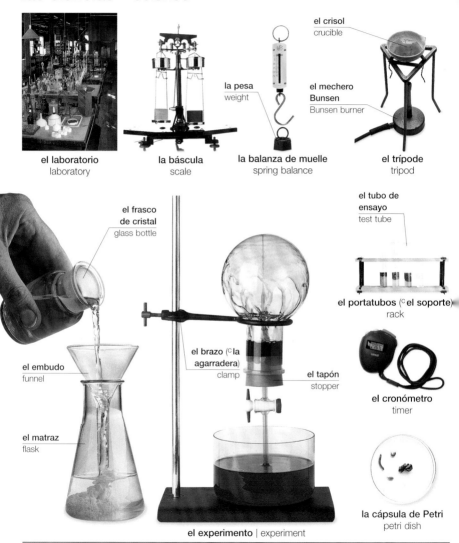

el laboratorio
laboratory

la báscula
scale

la pesa
weight

la balanza de muelle
spring balance

el crisol
crucible

el mechero Bunsen
Bunsen burner

el trípode
tripod

el frasco de cristal
glass bottle

el tubo de ensayo
test tube

el portatubos (ᶜel soporte)
rack

el embudo
funnel

el brazo (ᶜla agarradera)
clamp

el tapón
stopper

el cronómetro
timer

el matraz
flask

la cápsula de Petri
petri dish

el experimento | experiment

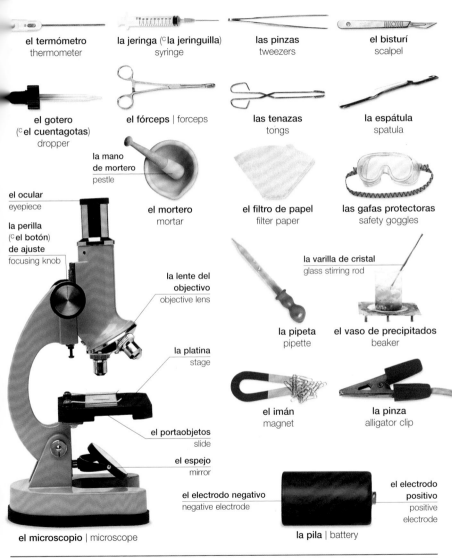

el termómetro
thermometer

la jeringa (^Cla jeringuilla)
syringe

las pinzas
tweezers

el bisturí
scalpel

el gotero
(^Cel cuentagotas)
dropper

el fórceps | forceps

las tenazas
tongs

la espátula
spatula

la mano
de mortero
pestle

el mortero
mortar

el filtro de papel
filter paper

las gafas protectoras
safety goggles

el ocular
eyepiece

la perilla
(^Cel botón)
de ajuste
focusing knob

la lente del
objectivo
objective lens

la varilla de cristal
glass stirring rod

la pipeta
pipette

el vaso de precipitados
beaker

la platina
stage

el imán
magnet

la pinza
alligator clip

el portaobjetos
slide

el espejo
mirror

el electrodo negativo
negative electrode

el electrodo
positivo
positive
electrode

el microscopio | microscope

la pila | battery

la enseñanza superior • college

el campo
de deportes
playing field

el comedor
(^C el refectorio)
cafeteria

el centro
de salud
health center

la residencia
estudiantil
(^C el colegio
mayor)
residence hall

la secretaría
admissions
office

el campus | campus

el bibliotecario *m*
la bibliotecaria *f*
librarian

el mostrador
de préstamos
circulation desk

el librero (^C la
estantería)
bookshelf

el periódico
periodical

la revista
journal

la biblioteca | library

vocabulario • vocabulary

el préstamo loan	la información help desk	renovar renew (v)
reservar reserve (v)	pedir prestado (^C coger prestado) borrow (v)	el libro book
la lista de lecturas reading list		el título title
	la sala de lectura reading room	
la fecha de devolución due date		el pasillo aisle
	la credencial (^C la tarjeta de la biblioteca) library card	

el profesor *m*
la profesora *f*
professor

el estudiante de licenciatura *m*
la estudiante de licenciatura *f*
(ᶜel estudiante de grado *m*
la estudiante de grada *f*)
undergraduate

el graduado *m*
la graduada *f*
graduate

la toga
gown

el auditorio (ᶜel anfiteatro)
lecture hall

la ceremonia de graduación
graduation ceremony

las escuelas • schools

el modelo *m*
la modelo *f*
model

la escuela de Bellas Artes
art school

el conservatorio
music school

la academia de danza
dance school

---

vocabulario • vocabulary

la beca scholarship	**la investigación** research	**la tesina** dissertation	**la medicina** medicine	**la literatura** literature
el diploma diploma	**el doctorado** doctorate	**el departamento** department	**la zoología** zoology	**las ciencias políticas** political science
la carrera degree	**la tesis** thesis	**el derecho** law	**la física** physics	**la historia del arte** art history
el estudiante de posgrado *m* **la estudiante de posgrado** *f* postgraduate	**la maestría** (ᶜel máster) master's	**la ingeniería** engineering	**la filosofía** philosophy	**las ciencias económicas** economics

el trabajo
work

la oficina • office (1)

el portaplumas
(C el portabolígrafos)
desktop organizer

la computadora
(C el ordenador portátil)
laptop

la pantalla
monitor

el cuaderno
notebook

la bandeja
de salida
out-tray

la bandeja de
entrada
in-tray

el cajón
drawer

el escritorio
desk

la silla
giratoria
swivel chair

el bote de basura
(C la papelera)
wastebasket

el archivero
(C el archivador)
filing cabinet

el equipo de oficina • office equipment

la bandeja
para el papel
paper tray

la impresora
printer

la destructora de papel
shredder

vocabulario • vocabulary	
imprimir print (v)	**ampliar** enlarge (v)
fotocopiar copy (v)	**reducir** reduce (v)

Necesito sacar (C hacer) unas copias.
I need to make some copies.

os materiales de oficina • office supplies

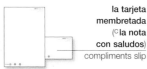

el membrete
letterhead

la tarjeta membretada
(ᶜ **la nota con saludos**)
compliments slip

el sobre
envelope

la caja archivador
box file

la tabla con portapapeles
(ᶜ **la tablilla con sujetapapeles**)
clipboard

la libreta (ᶜ **el bloc de apuntes**)
notepad

el rótulo
tab

el colgante
(ᶜ **el archivador suspendido**)
hanging file

el divisor
divider

la carpeta de acordeón
expanding file

la carpeta de argollas
(ᶜ **de anillas**)
binder

la agenda
personal organizer

las grapas
staples

la engrapadora
(ᶜ **la grapadora**)
stapler

la cinta scotch
(ᶜ **el papel celo**)
tape

el portacinta
(ᶜ **el soporte del papel celo**)
tape dispenser

la perforadora
hole punch

el cojín de la tinta
(ᶜ **la almohadilla de la tinta**)
ink pad

el sello
rubber stamp

la liga
(ᶜ **la goma elástica**)
rubber band

la pinza
(ᶜ **el clip**)
bulldog clip

la chinche
(ᶜ **la chincheta**)
thumbtack

el clip
(ᶜ **el sujetapapeles**)
paper clip

el tablón de anuncios
bulletin board

la oficina • office (2)

la propuesta
proposal

el gerente *m*
la gerente *f*
manager

el ejecutivo *m*
la ejecutiva *f*
executive

el pizarrón
(ᶜ el rotafolio)
flip chart

el caballete
easel

la minuta
(ᶜ el acta)
minutes

el reporte
(ᶜ el informe)
report

la junta (ᶜ la reunión) | meeting

vocabulario • vocabulary	
el orden del día agenda	**asistir** attend (v)
la sala de juntas (ᶜ reuniones) meeting room	**presidir** chair (v)

¿A qué hora es la junta (ᶜ la reunión)?
What time is the meeting?

¿Cuál es su horario de oficina?
What are your office hours?

el orador *m*
la oradora *f*
speaker

la presentación | presentation

os negocios • business

el hombre de negocios
businessman / businessperson

la mujer de negocios
businesswoman / businessperson

la comida de negocios
business lunch

el viaje de negocios
business trip

la cita
appointment

el director general *m*
la directora general *f*
CEO

el cliente *m*
la clienta *f*
client

el calendario digital | digital calendar

el trato | business deal

---

vocabulario • vocabulary

la empresa
company

el personal
staff

el departamento de ventas
sales department

el departamento legal
legal department

la oficina central
head office

la nómina
payroll

el departamento de contabilidad
accounting department

el departamento de atención al cliente
customer service department

la sucursal
regional office

el sueldo
salary

el departamento de márketing
marketing department

el departamento de recursos humanos
human resources department

---

la computadora (^C el ordenador) • computer

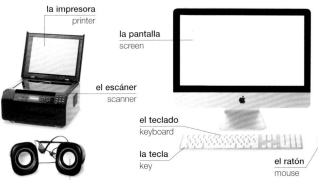

la impresora
printer

la pantalla
screen

el escáner
scanner

la computadora
(^C el ordenador
portátil)
laptop

el teclado
keyboard

la tecla
key

el ratón
mouse

la bocina
(^C el altavoz)
speaker

los audífonos bluetooth
(^C el auricular bluetooth)
bluetooth headset

la cámara web
webcam

el router (^C el rúter)
router

la llave de memoria
memory stick

vocabulario • vocabulary

la memoria memory	el software software	el servidor server
la RAM RAM	la aplicación application	el puerto port
los bytes bytes	el programa program	el precesador processor
el sistema system	la red network	el cable de alimentación power cord
el hardware hardware	conectar connect (v)	

la cámara webel
disco duro externo
external hard drive

el paquete de pilas
battery pack

el cable
de carga
charging
cable

el teléfono inteligente
smartphone

la tablet
tablet

el escritorio • desktop

barra del menú
menu bar

la fuente
font

la barra de
herramientas
(° la barra
de acceso)
toolbar

el icono
icon

la ventana
window

el archivo
(° el fichero)
file

la carpeta
folder

el basurero
(° la papelera)
trash

el internet • Internet

el sitio web
website

el navegador
browser

navegar
browse (v)

el correo electrónico • email

la bandeja
de entrada
inbox

la dirección electrónica
email address

---

vocabulario • vocabulary

instalar install (v)	almacenamiento en la nube cloud storage	en línea online	bajar download (v)	la contraseña password	guardar save (v)
recibir receive (v)	el proveedor de servicios service provider	entrar en el sistema log on (v)	el documento adjunto attachment	enviar send (v)	buscar search (v)

---

los medios de comunicación • media

el estudio de televisión • television studio

el plató
set

el presentador *m*
la presentadora *f*
host

el reflector (^Cel foco)
light

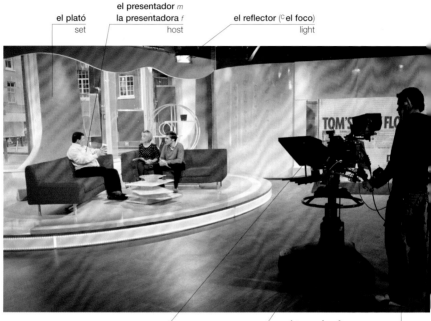

la cámara
camera

la grúa de la cámara
camera crane

el camarógrafo *m*
la camarógrafa *f*
(^Cel cámara *m* / la cámara *f*)
camera operator

---

vocabulario • vocabulary

el canal channel	el documental documentary	la prensa press	la telenovela soap opera	el concurso game show	en directo live
la programación programming	las noticias news	la serie televisiva television series	transmitir (^Cemitir) broadcast (v)	las caricaturas (^Clos dibujos animados) cartoon	pregrabado (^Cen diferido) prerecorded

---

el entrevistador *m*
la entrevistadora *f*
interviewer

el reportero *m*
la reportera *f*
reporter

el teleprompter
(^c**el autocue**)
teleprompter

el presentador *m*
la presentadora *f*
anchor

los actores *m*
las actrices *f*
actors

el micrófono de aire
(^c**la jirafa**) | sound boom

la pizarra (^c**la claqueta**)
clapper board

el plató de rodaje
movie set

la radio • radio

el técnico de sonido *m*
la técnica de sonido *f*
sound technician

la consola
(^c**la mesa
de mezclas**)
mixing desk

el micrófono
microphone

el estudio de grabación | recording studio

vocabulario • vocabulary	
la estación de radio radio station	**la transmisión** (^c**la emisión**) broadcast
el DJ *m* **la DJ** *f* DJ	**analógico** *m* **analógica** *f* analogue
la longitud de onda wavelength	**digital** digital
la frecuencia frequency	
el volumen volume	
sintonizar tune (v)	

el derecho • law

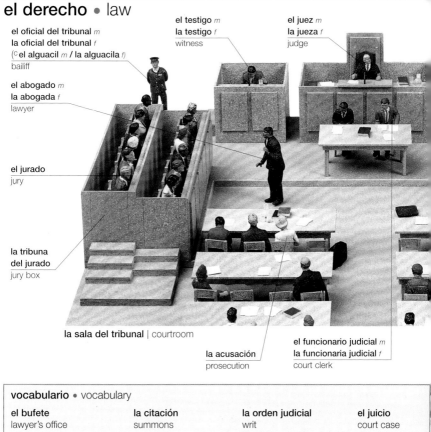

el oficial del tribunal *m*
la oficial del tribunal *f*
(ᶜ **el alguacil** *m* **/ la alguacila** *f*)
bailiff

el abogado *m*
la abogada *f*
lawyer

el jurado
jury

la tribuna del jurado
jury box

el testigo *m*
la testigo *f*
witness

el juez *m*
la jueza *f*
judge

la sala del tribunal | courtroom

la acusación
prosecution

el funcionario judicial *m*
la funcionaria judicial *f*
court clerk

---

vocabulario • vocabulary

el bufete lawyer's office	**la citación** summons	**la orden judicial** writ	**el juicio** court case
la asesoría jurídica legal advice	**la declaración** statement	**la fecha del juicio** court date	**el cargo** charge
el cliente *m* **la clienta** *f* client	**la orden judicial** warrant	**la súplica** (ᶜ **el alegato**) plea	**el acusado** *m* **la acusada** *f* accused

el taquígrafo *m*
la taquígrafa *f*
stenographer

el criminal *m*
la criminal *f*
criminal

el sospechoso *m*
la sospechosa *f*
suspect

la defensa
defense

el acusado *m*
la acusada *f*
defendant

el retrato hablado
(^C el retrato robot)
composite sketch

los antecedentes
criminal record

el guardia de la prisión *m* / la guardia de la prisión *f*
(^C el funcionario de prisiones *m* / la funcionaria de prisiones *f*)
prison guard

la celda
cell

la cárcel
prison

vocabulario • vocabulary

el veredicto verdict	**absuelto** *m* **absuelta** *f* acquitted	**la fianza** bail	**Quiero ver a un abogado.** I want to see a lawyer.
inocente innocent	**la sentencia** sentence	**la apelación** appeal	**¿Dónde está el juzgado?** Where is the courthouse?
culpable guilty	**la evidencia** (^C**la prueba**) evidence	**la libertad condicional** parole	**¿Puedo pagar la fianza?** Can I post bail?

la granja • farm (1)

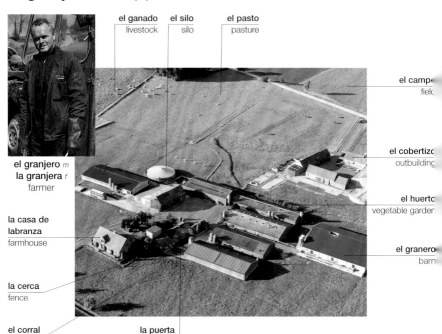

el ganado
livestock

el silo
silo

el pasto
pasture

el camp•
fiel•

el cobertiz•
outbuilding

el huert•
vegetable garden

el graner•
barn

el granjero *m*
la granjera *f*
farmer

la casa de
labranza
farmhouse

la cerca
fence

el corral
farmyard

la puerta
gate

el tractor | tractor

la cosechadora | combine

os tipos de granja • types of farms

la cosecha
crop

la granja de tierras cultivables
crop farm

la vaquería
dairy farm

el rebaño
flock

la granja de ganado ovino
sheep farm

la granja avícola
poultry farm

la viña (ᶜla vid)
vine

la granja de ganado porcino
pig farm

el criadero de peces (ᶜla piscifactoría)
fish farm

la granja de frutales
fruit farm

el viñedo
vineyard

---

las actividades • actions

el surco
furrow

arar
plow (v)

sembrar
sow (v)

ordeñar
milk (v)

alimentar (ᶜdar de comer)
feed (v)

regar | water (v)

cosechar | harvest (v)

vocabulario • vocabulary		
el herbicida herbicide	**la manada** herd	**el comedero** trough
el pesticida pesticide	**el silo** silo	**plantar** plant (v)

---

la granja • farm (2)

los cultivos (^C las cosechas) • crops

el trigo
wheat

el maíz
corn

la cebada
barley

la colza
rapeseed

el girasol
sunflower

la paca
(^C la bala)
bale

el heno
hay

la alfalfa
alfalfa

el tabaco
tobacco

el arroz
rice

el té
tea

el café
coffee

el lino
flax

la caña de azúcar
sugarcane

el algodón
cotton

el espantapájaros
scarecrow

el ganado • livestock

el chanchito
(ᶜel lechón)
piglet

el puerco (ᶜel cerdo)
pig

el ternero
calf

la vaca
cow

el toro
bull

la oveja
sheep

el cordero
lamb

el cabrito
kid

la cabra
goat

el potro
foal

el caballo
horse

el burro
donkey

el pollito
(ᶜel polluelo)
chick

la gallina
chicken

el gallo
rooster

el guajolote (ᶜel pavo)
turkey

el patito
duckling

el pato
duck

el establo
stable

el redil
pen

el gallinero
chicken coop

el chiquero (ᶜla pocilga)
pigsty

la construcción
construction

la pared
wall

la viga de
madera
beam

el andamio
scaffolding

la tarima
(ᶜ el palet)
pallet

la viga
del tejado
rafter

la obra
construction site

la ventana
window

la escalera
ladder

la viga
de acero
girder

el casco
hard hat

el cinturón de
las herramientas
toolbelt

el
cemento
cement

construir
build (v)

el trabajador de la construcción *m*
la trabajadora de la construcción *f*
(ᶜ el obrero *m* / la obrera *f*)
construction worker

la mezcladora de cemento
(ᶜ **la hormigonera**)
cement mixer

os materiales • materials

el ladrillo
brick

la madera
lumber

la teja
roof tile

el bloque de hormigón
cinder block

las herramientas • tools

la argamasa
mortar

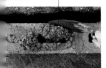
la paleta
trowel

el nivel
level

el mango
handle

el mazo
sledgehammer

el zapapico
(C **el pico**)
pickax

la pala
shovel

la maquinaria
machinery

la aplanadora
(C **la apisonadora**)
road roller

el camión de volteo
(C **el camión volquete**)
dump truck

el soporte
support

el gancho
hook

la grúa | crane

las obras viales (C las obras)
roadwork

el asfalto
asphalt

el cono
cone

el martillo neumático
jackhammer

el revestimiento
resurfacing

la pala mecánica
(C **la excavadora mecánica**)
excavator

las profesiones • occupations (1)

el carpintero m
la carpintera f
carpenter

el electricista m
la electricista f
electrician

el plomero m **la plomera** f
(ᶜ **el fontanero** m / **la fontanera** f)
plumber

el albañil
construction
worker

el mecánico m
la mecánica f
mechanic

el carnicero m
la carnicera f
butcher

el pescador m
la pescadora f
fisherman / fisherwoman

el florista m
la florista f
florist

el joyero m
la joyera f
jeweler

el jardinero m
la jardinera f
gardener

el estilista m / **la estilista** f
(ᶜ **el peluquero** m / **la peluquera** f)
hairdresser

el peluquero m
la peluquera f
(ᶜ **el barbero** m
la barbera f)
barber

el vendedor m
la vendedora f
(ᶜ **el dependiente** m
la dependienta f)
salesperson

el instructor de manejo m
la instructora de manejo f
(ᶜ **el profesor de autoescuela** m
la profesora de autoescuela f)
driving instructor

la
aspiradora
vacuum
cleaner

el limpiador m
la limpiadora f
cleaner

el perito m
la perito f
surveyor

el farmacéutico _m_
la farmacéutica _f_
pharmacist

el optometrista _m_
la optometrista _f_
(C el óptico _m_ / la óptica _f_)
optometrist

la mascarilla
mask

el dentista _m_
la dentista _f_
dentist

el doctor _m_
la doctora _f_
doctor

el enfermero _m_
la enfermera _f_
nurse

el veterinario _m_
la veterinaria _f_
veterinarian

el fisioterapeuta _m_
la fisioterapeuta _f_
physiotherapist

el bombero _m_
la bombera _f_
firefighter

el uniforme
uniform

el soldado _m_
la soldado _f_
soldier

el policía _m_
la policía _f_
police officer

placa de
ntificación
dge

el guardia de
seguridad _m_ / la
guardia de seguridad _f_
security guard

el marinero _m_
la marinera _f_
sailor

vocabulario • vocabulary

el ejecutivo de publicidad _m_
la ejecutiva de publicidad _f_
(C el responsable de marketing _m_
la responsable de marketing _f_)
marketing executive

el ejecutivo de relaciones públicas _m_
la ejecutiva de relaciones públicas _f_
(C el responsable de relaciones públicas (RR. PP.) _m_
la responsable de relaciones públicas (RR. PP.) _f_)
public relations executive (PR)

el asistente de personal _m_ / la asistente de personal _f_
personal assistant (PA)

el desarrollador de aplicaciones _m_
la desarrolladora de aplicaciones _f_
app developer

el emprendedor _m_ / la emprendedora _f_
(C el empresario _m_ / la empresaria _f_)
entrepreneur

el diseñador web _m_   el intérprete _m_
la diseñadora web _f_   la intérprete _f_
web designer   interpreter

las profesiones • occupations (2)

el abogado *m*
la abogadala *f*
lawyer

el contador *m* / la contadora *f*
(^cel contable *m*
la contable *f*)
accountant

la maqueta
model

el arquitecto *m*
la arquitecta *f*
architect

el analista de datos *m*
la analista de datos *f*
data analyst

el científico *m*
la científica *f*
scientist

el maestro *m*
la maestra *f*
teacher

el agente immobiliario *m*
la agente inmobiliaria *f*
real estate agent

el recepcionista *m*
la recepcionista *f*
receptionist

la cartera
mailbag

el cartero *m*
la cartera *f*
mail carrier

el conductor de autobús *m*
la conductora de autobús *f*
bus driver

el chófer *m* / la chófer *f*
(^cel camionero *m*
la camionera *f*)
truck driver

el taxista *m*
la taxista *f*
taxi driver

el piloto *m*
la piloto *f*
pilot

el sobrecargo *m*
la sobrecargo *f*
(^cla azafata *m* / la azafata *f*)
flight attendant

el agente de viajes *m*
la agente de viajes *f*
travel agent

el gorro de
cocinero
chef's hat

el chef *m*
la chef *f*
chef

el tutú
tutu

el músico *m*
la música *f*
musician

el bailarín *m*
la bailarina *f*
dancer

el actor *m*
la actriz *f*
actor

el cantante *m*
la cantante *f*
singer

el mesero *m* **/ la mesera** *f*
(ᶜ**el camarero** *m*
la camarera *f*)
server

el barman *m*
la barman *f*
bartender

el entrenador personal *m*
la entrenadora personal *f*
personal trainer

el escultor *m*
la escultora *f*
sculptor

las notas
notes

el pintor *m*
la pintora *f*
painter

el fotógrafo *m*
la fotógrafa *f*
photographer

el presentador *m*
la presentadora *f*
anchor

el periodista *m*
la periodista *f*
journalist

el editor *m*
la editora *f*
editor

el diseñador *m*
la diseñadora *f*
designer

el modisto *m*
la modista *f*
dressmaker

el sastre
tailor

el transporte
transportation

las carreteras • roads

el paso a desnivel
(ᶜ el paso
subterráneo)
underpass

las señales de piso
(ᶜ las señales
horizontales)
road markings

la rampa
de salida
(ᶜ la vía de salida)
off-ramp

el muro
de división
(ᶜ la mediana)
median strip

el acotamiento
(ᶜ el arcén)
shoulder

el tránsito
(ᶜ el tráfico)
traffic

el carril central
middle lane

el carril de baja
(ᶜ el carril para
el tráfico lento)
driving lane

la autopista
freeway

el carril
izquierdo
(ᶜ el carril de
adelantamiento)
passing lane

la entrada
(ᶜ la vía de acceso)
on-ramp

el puente
(ᶜ el paso
elevado)
overpass

el semáforo
traffic light

el paso de
peatones
crosswalk

el camion
truck

el crucero
interchange

el teléfono
de emergencia
emergency phone

el estacionamiento
(^{C} el aparcamiento)
para minusválidos
disabled parking

el tráfico
(^{C} el atasco de tráfico)
traffic jam

el parquímetro
parking meter

el policía de tránsito *m*
la policía de tránsito *f*
(^{C} el policía de tráfico *m*
la policía de tráfico *f*)
traffic police officer

vocabulario • vocabulary

la desviación (^{C} el desvío)
detour

estacionar (^{C} aparcar)
park (v)

la glorieta
roundabout

meter reversa
(^{C} dar marcha atrás)
reverse (v)

manejar (^{C} conducir)
drive (v)

rebasar (^{C} adelantar)
pass (v)

las obras
roadwork

el muro de
contención
(^{C} la barrera
de seguridad)
guardrail

remolcar
tow away (v)

la autovía
divided highway

la calle de
sentido único
one-way street

la caseta
de cobro
tollbooth

¿Es ésta la
carretera
hacia... ?
Is this the
road to... ?

¿Dónde
me puedo
estacionar
(^{C} aparcar)?
Where can
I park?

las señales de tránsito (^{C} trafíco) • road signs

prohibido
el paso
do not enter

el límite
de velocidad
speed limit

peligro
hazard

prohibido
parar
no stopping

no dar vuelta (^{C} no
torcer) a la derecha
no right turn

el autobús • bus

el asiento
del conductor
driver's seat

la barandilla
handrail

la ventanilla
(ᶜla ventana)
window

la rueda
delantera
front wheel

la rueda trasera
rear wheel

el portaequipajes
luggage hold

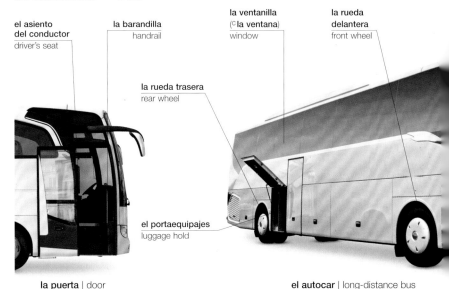

la puerta | door

el autocar | long-distance bus

los tipos de autobuses • types of buses

el número de ruta
route number

el chófer *m*
la chofer *f*
(ᶜel conductor
de autobús *m*
la conductor
de autobús *f*)
driver

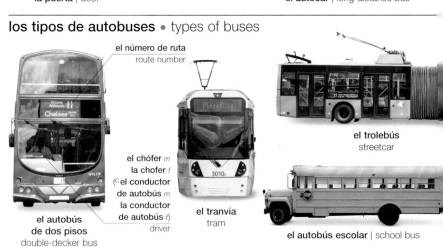

el autobús
de dos pisos
double-decker bus

el tranvía
tram

el trolebús
streetcar

el autobús escolar | school bus

la puerta automática
automatic door

el botón
de parada
stop button

el boleto (ᶜel
billete) de autobús
bus ticket

el timbre
bell

la estación de autobuses
bus station

la parada
de autobús
bus stop

vocabulario • vocabulary

la tarifa
fare

el horario
schedule

la marquesina
bus shelter

la rampa para sillas
de ruedas
wheelchair access

¿Para usted en… ?
Do you stop at… ?

¿Qué autobús va a… ?
Which bus goes to… ?

el microbús
minibus

el autobús turístico | tour bus

el autobús directo (ᶜde enlace)
shuttle bus

el carro (^cel coche) • car (1)

el exterior • exterior

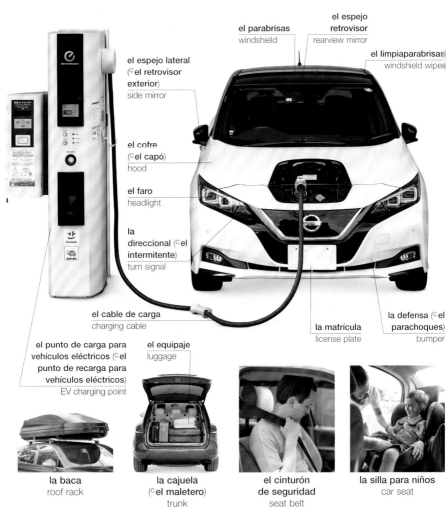

el parabrisas
windshield

el espejo retrovisor
rearview mirror

el limpiaparabrisas
windshield wiper

el espejo lateral
(^cel retrovisor exterior)
side mirror

el cofre
(^cel capó)
hood

el faro
headlight

la direccional (^cel intermitente)
turn signal

el cable de carga
charging cable

el punto de carga para vehículos eléctricos (^cel punto de recarga para vehículos eléctricos)
EV charging point

el equipaje
luggage

la matrícula
license plate

la defensa (^cel parachoques)
bumper

la baca
roof rack

la cajuela
(^cel maletero)
trunk

el cinturón de seguridad
seat belt

la silla para niños
car seat

os modelos • types

el coche eléctrico
electric car

la puerta
door

el carro (ᶜel coche de cinco puertas) de cinco puertas
hatchback

el carro familiar
(ᶜel turismo)
sedan

la rueda
wheel

la camioneta
(ᶜel coche ranchera)
station wagon

el convertible
el coche descapotable)
convertible

el coche deportivo
sports car

la minivan
(ᶜel monovolumen)
minivan

la doble tracción
(ᶜel todoterreno)
four-wheel drive

la llanta (ᶜel neumático)
tire

el auto de época (ᶜel coche de época)
vintage

la limusina
limousine

la gasolinera • gas station

la bomba
(ᶜel surtidor)
gas pump

el precio
price

la zona de abastecimiento
entryway

vocabulario • vocabulary		
el aceite oil	el diesel diesel	el anticongelante antifreeze
la gasolina gasoline	con plomo leaded	el auto-lavado (ᶜel lavadero de coches) car wash
sin plomo unleaded	el taller garage	el líquido limpiaparabrisas windshield washer fluid

Llénelo por favor. (ᶜLleno, por favor.)
Fill it up, please.

el carro (^Cel coche) • car (2)

el interior • interior

			el seguro	la manij
			(^Cel pestillo)	(^Cel tirador
el asiento trasero	el reposabrazos	el reposacabezas	door lock	handl
backseat	armrest	headrest		

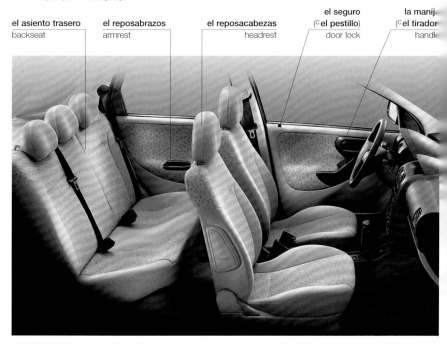

vocabulario • vocabulary

dos puertas	de cuatro	automático	el freno	el acelerador
two-door	**puertas**	automatic	brake	accelerator
	four-door			
de tres		el	el	el aire
puertas	**manual**	**encendido**	**embrague**	**acondicionado**
hatchback	manual	ignition	clutch	air-conditioning

¿Me puede decir cómo se	¿Dónde hay un	¿Se puede estacionar
va... ?	estacionamiento (^Cparking)?	(^Caparcar) aquí?
Can you tell me the way to... ?	Where is the parking lot?	Can I park here?

español • english

os controles • controls

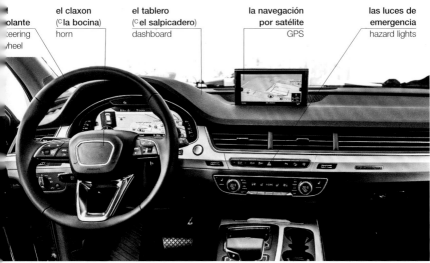

olante
steering
wheel

el claxon
(C **la bocina**)
horn

el tablero
(C **el salpicadero**)
dashboard

la navegación por satélite
GPS

las luces de emergencia
hazard lights

el volante a la izquierda | left-hand drive

la radio del coche
car stereo

el tacómetro
(C **el cuentarrevoluciones**)
tachometer

el velocímetro
(C **el indicador de velocidad**)
speedometer

el indicador de la gasolina
fuel gauge

el indicador de temperatura
temperature gauge

la palanca
(C **el conmutador**)
de luces
light switch

la calefacción
heater controls

el odómetro
(C **el cuenta-
kilómetros**)
odometer

la palanca de velocidades
(C **de cambios**)
gearshift

la bolsa de aire
(C **el airbag**)
air bag

el volante a la derecha | right-hand drive

español • english

el carro (^Cel coche) • car (3)

la mecánica • mechanics

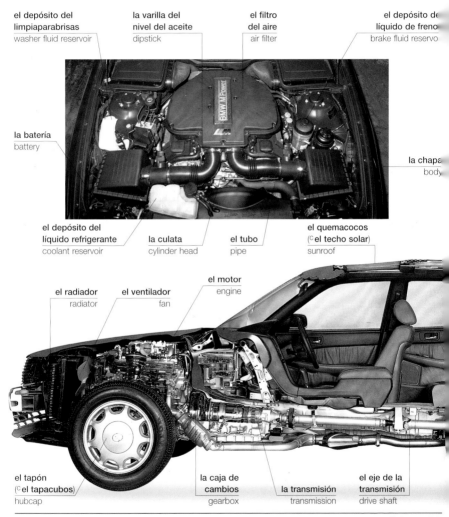

el depósito del limpiaparabrisas
washer fluid reservoir

la varilla del nivel del aceite
dipstick

el filtro del aire
air filter

el depósito de líquido de freno
brake fluid reservoir

la batería
battery

la chapa
body

el depósito del líquido refrigerante
coolant reservoir

la culata
cylinder head

el tubo
pipe

el quemacocos (^Cel techo solar)
sunroof

el radiador
radiator

el ventilador
fan

el motor
engine

el tapón (^Cel tapacubos)
hubcap

la caja de cambios
gearbox

la transmisión
transmission

el eje de la transmisión
drive shaft

a ponchadura (^C el pinchazo) • flat tire

a llanta de refacción
la rueda de repuesto)
pare tire

a llave
re iron

los birlos (^C los tornillos)
lug nuts

el gato
jack

cambiar una llanta (^C una rueda)
change a tire (v)

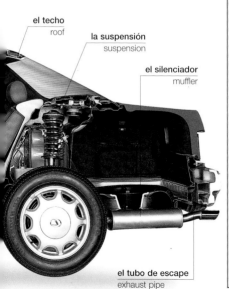

el techo
roof

la suspensión
suspension

el silenciador
muffler

el tubo de escape
exhaust pipe

vocabulario • vocabulary

el accidente de coche car accident	**el tanque de la gasolina** gas tank
la avería breakdown	**el turbo** turbocharger
el seguro insurance	**el distribuidor** distributor
la grúa tow truck	**el ralentí** timing
el mecánico mechanic	**el chasis** chassis
la presión del neumático tire pressure	**la banda del disco** (^C **la correa del disco**) timing belt
la caja de fusibles fuse box	**el freno de mano** parking brake
la bujía spark plug	**la banda del ventilador** (^C **la correa del ventilador**) fan belt
el alternador alternator	

Se descompuso el carro.
(^C **Mi coche se ha averiado.**)
My car has broken down.

El carro no arranca.
(^C **Mi coche no arranca.**)
My car won't start.

la motocicleta • motorcycle

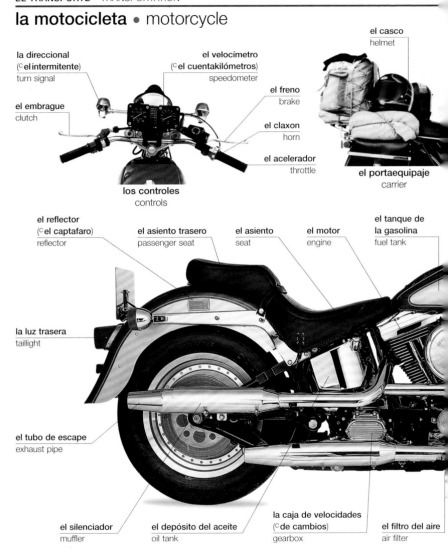

el casco
helmet

la direccional
(ᶜ el intermitente)
turn signal

el velocímetro
(ᶜ el cuentakilómetros)
speedometer

el freno
brake

el embrague
clutch

el claxon
horn

el acelerador
throttle

el portaequipaje
carrier

los controles
controls

el reflector
(ᶜ el captafaro)
reflector

el asiento trasero
passenger seat

el asiento
seat

el motor
engine

el tanque de
la gasolina
fuel tank

la luz trasera
taillight

el tubo de escape
exhaust pipe

el silenciador
muffler

el depósito del aceite
oil tank

la caja de velocidades
(ᶜ de cambios)
gearbox

el filtro del aire
air filter

español • english

visera
sor

a cinta
eflectante
eflector strap

el traje de cuero
leathers

la rodillera
kneepad

el equipo | clothing

el faro
headlight

la suspensión
suspension

la salpicadera
(ᶜ el guardabarros)
fender

el pedal de
los frenos
brake pedal

el eje
axle

la llanta
(ᶜ el neumático)
tire

los tipos • types

la moto de carreras | racing bike

el parabrisas
windshield

la moto de carretera | tourer

la motocross (ᶜ **la moto de cross**)
dirt bike

el soporte
stand

la vespa | scooter

la bicicleta · bicycle

el tándem
tandem

la bicicleta de carreras
racing bike

la bicicleta de montaña
mountain bike

el asiento (ᶜ el sillín)
saddle

el poste del asiento
(ᶜ el soporte del sillín)
seat post

el cuadro
frame

la botella del agua
water bottle

el freno
brake

el eje
hub

los cambios
(ᶜ las marchas)
gears

el casco
helmet

el rin (ᶜ la llanta)
rim

la llanta
(ᶜ la cubierta)
tire

la cadena
chain

la estrella (ᶜ el diente de la rueda)
cog

el pedal
pedal

la banda del calzapié (ᶜ la correa del calzapié)
toe strap

la bicicleta adaptada
paracyle

la bicicleta plegable
folding bike

el carril de bicicletas | bike lane

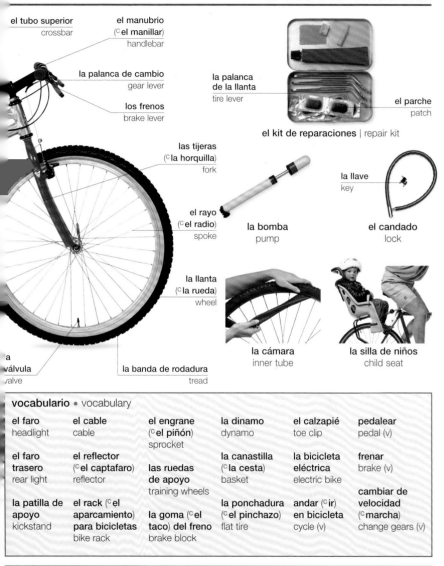

el tubo superior
crossbar

el manubrio
(ᶜ el manillar)
handlebar

la palanca de cambio
gear lever

los frenos
brake lever

la palanca
de la llanta
tire lever

el parche
patch

el kit de reparaciones | repair kit

las tijeras
(ᶜ la horquilla)
fork

la llave
key

el rayo
(ᶜ el radio)
spoke

la bomba
pump

el candado
lock

la llanta
(ᶜ la rueda)
wheel

la cámara
inner tube

la silla de niños
child seat

la
válvula
valve

la banda de rodadura
tread

vocabulario • vocabulary

el faro headlight	**el cable** cable	**el engrane** (ᶜ **el piñón**) sprocket	**la dinamo** dynamo	**el calzapié** toe clip	**pedalear** pedal (v)
el faro trasero rear light	**el reflector** (ᶜ **el captafaro**) reflector	**las ruedas de apoyo** training wheels	**la canastilla** (ᶜ **la cesta**) basket	**la bicicleta eléctrica** electric bike	**frenar** brake (v)
la patilla de apoyo kickstand	**el rack** (ᶜ **el aparcamiento**) **para bicicletas** bike rack	**la goma** (ᶜ **el taco**) **del freno** brake block	**la ponchadura** (ᶜ **el pinchazo**) flat tire	**andar** (ᶜ **ir**) **en bicicleta** cycle (v)	**cambiar de velocidad** (ᶜ **marcha**) change gears (v)

el tren • train

el andén
platform

la vía
track

el número de
andén
platform number

el vagón
railcar

el viajero de
cercanías /
la viajera
de cercanías
commuter

la estación de tren | train station

los tipos de tren • types of train

el tren de vapor
steam train

la locomotora
engine

la cabina del
conductor
engineer's
cab

el vía (ᶜel raíl)
rail

el tren diesel | diesel train

el tren eléctrico
electric train

el tren de alta velocidad
high-speed train

el monorriel (ᶜel monorraíl)
monorail

el metro
subway

el tranvía
tram

el tren de carga
(ᶜel tren de mercancías)
freight train

el portaequipajes
luggage rack

la ventanilla
window

la puerta
door

el vagón
compartment

el altavoz (ᶜel sistema de megafonía)
public address system

el asiento
seat

el horario
schedule

el boleto (ᶜel billete)
ticket

la barrera
ticket gates

el vagón restaurante | dining car

el vestíbulo | concourse

el cochecama
sleeping compartment

vocabulario • vocabulary

la red ferroviaria railroad network	**el plano del metro** subway map	**la taquilla** ticket office	**el riel electrificado** live rail
el tren intercity express train	**el retraso** delay	**cambiar** transfer (v)	**la señal** signal
la hora pico (ᶜla hora punta) rush hour	**el precio** fare	**la persona que revisa los boletos** *m/f* ticket inspector	**el freno de emergencia** emergency lever

el avión • aircraft

el avión de pasajeros • airliner

la nariz
(ᶜ el morro)
nose

la cabina
de mando
cockpit

el motor
engine

el fuselaje
fuselage

el ala
wing

la col
ta

el timón
rudde

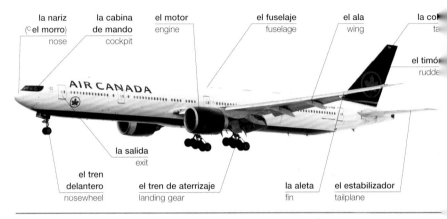

la salida
exit

el tren
delantero
nosewheel

el tren de aterrizaje
landing gear

la aleta
fin

el estabilizador
tailplane

la cabina • cabin

el sobrecargo *m*
la sobrecargo *f*
(ᶜ el azafato *m*
la azafata *f*)
flight attendant

el compartimento
portaequipajes
overhead bin

el ventilador
air vent

la ventanilla
window

la luz de lectura
reading light

la fila
row

el asiento
seat

la mesa plegable
(ᶜ la bandeja)
tray table

el respaldo
seat back

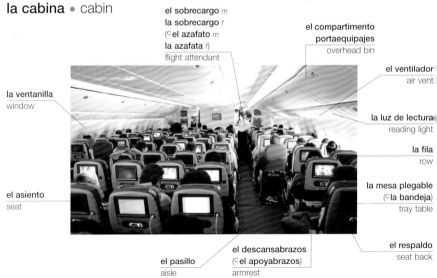

el pasillo
aisle

el descansabrazos
(ᶜ el apoyabrazos)
armrest

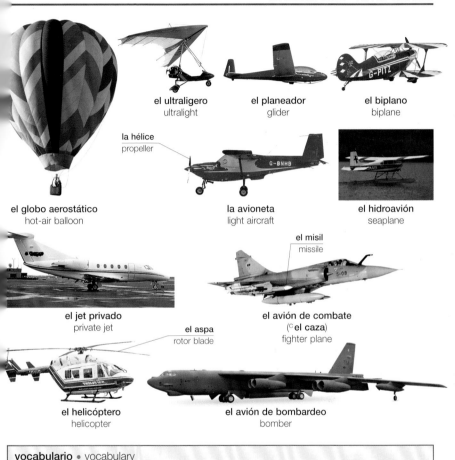

el ultraligero
ultralight

el planeador
glider

el biplano
biplane

la hélice
propeller

el globo aerostático
hot-air balloon

la avioneta
light aircraft

el hidroavión
seaplane

el misil
missile

el jet privado
private jet

el avión de combate
(ᶜel caza)
fighter plane

el aspa
rotor blade

el helicóptero
helicopter

el avión de bombardeo
bomber

vocabulario • vocabulary

el piloto _m_ **la piloto** _f_ piloto	**despegar** take off (v)	**aterrizar** land (v)	**la clase turista** economy class	**el equipaje de mano** carry-on luggage
el copiloto _m_ **la copiloto** _f_ copiloto	**volar** fly (v)	**la altitud** altitude	**la clase preferente** business class	**el cinturón de seguridad** seat belt

el aeropuerto • airport

el área de estacionamient
apr⊂

el remolque del equipaj
baggage traile

la pasarel⊂
jetway

el vehículo de servicio
service vehicle

el avión de línea | airliner

---

vocabulario • vocabulary

la pista
runway

la terminal
terminal

**el vuelo
internacional**
international flight

el vuelo nacional
domestic flight

la conexión
connection

la aduana
customs

**el número
de vuelo**
flight number

inmigración
immigration

**la recepción
de equipaje**
(ᶜ **el mostrador
del equipaje**)
baggage drop

**el exceso
de equipaje**
excess baggage

la seguridad
security

la banda transportadora
(ᶜ **la cinta de equipajes**)
baggage carousel

la máquina de rayos x
X-ray machine

el folleto de viajes
travel brochure

las vacaciones
vacation

reservar un vuelo
book a flight (v)

la torre de control
control tower (v)

hacer check-in
(ᶜ **facturar**)
check in (v)

---

l equipaje
le mano
carry-on
luggage

el carrito
(ᶜ el carro)
cart

el equipaje
luggage

el mostrador de check-in
(ᶜ el mostrador de facturación)
check-in desk

la visa
(ᶜ el visado)
visa

el pasaporte | passport

el control
de pasaportes
passport control

la tarjeta de embarque
boarding pass

el número de
puerta de embarque
gate number

la sala de embarque
departure lounge

las salidas
departures

las llegadas
arrivals

el destino
destination

la pantalla de información
information screen

la puerta electrónica
(ᶜ la puerta de embarque
electrónica)
eGate

el duty-free (ᶜ la tienda
libre de impuestos)
duty-free store

la recogida de
equipajes
baggage claim

el sitio de taxis
(ᶜ la parada de taxis)
taxi stand

la renta de carros
(ᶜ el alquiler de coches)
car rental

el barco · ship

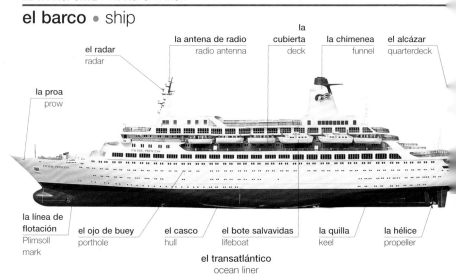

la antena de radio
radio antenna

el radar
radar

la
cubierta
deck

la chimenea
funnel

el alcázar
quarterdeck

la proa
prow

la línea de
flotación
Plimsoll
mark

el ojo de buey
porthole

el casco
hull

el bote salvavidas
lifeboat

la quilla
keel

la hélice
propeller

el transatlántico
ocean liner

el puente
bridge

la sala de máquinas
engine room

el camarote
cabin

la cocina
galley

vocabulario · vocabulary

el muelle
dock

el puerto
port

la pasarela
gangway

el ancla
anchor

el noray
bollard

el cabrestante
windlass

la barca de remos
rowboat

la piragua
canoe

la lancha de motor
(°la lancha motora)
speedboat

el capitán *m*
la capitana *f*
captain

otras barcos • other boats

el ferry
ferry

el motor fueraborda
outboard motor

la zódiac
inflatable dinghy

el hidrodeslizador
hydrofoil

el yate
yacht

el catamarán
catamaran

el remolcador
tugboat

el aerodeslizador
hovercraft

el barco carguero (ᶜ**el buque portacontenedores**)
container ship

la vela
sail

el barco de vela
sailboat

la bodega
hold

el buque de carga
freighter

el buque tanque
(ᶜ**el petrolero**)
oil tanker

el portaaviones
aircraft carrier

el barco de guerra
battleship

la falsa torre
conning tower

el submarino
submarine

el puerto • port

la carga
cargo

la bodega
(^Cel almacén)
warehouse

la grúa
crane

el muelle
quay

las aduana
del puerto (^Cl
vía de acceso
customs house

la dársena
dock

la carretilla elevadora
forklift

el contenedor
container

el ferry
ferry

la terminal del ferry
ferry terminal

el pasajero *m*
la pasajera *f*
passenger

la ventanilla
de boletos
(^Cla ventanilla
de pasajes)
ticket office

el muelle comercial | container port

el muelle de pasajeros | passenger port

la red
net

el barco pesquero
(ᶜel barco de pesca)
fishing boat

el punto de amarre
mooring

el puerto deportivo
marina

el puerto pesquero (ᶜel puerto de pesca)
fishing port

el puerto
harbor

el embarcadero
pier

el espigón
jetty

el astillero
shipyard

la lámpara
lamp

el faro
lighthouse

la boya
buoy

vocabulario • vocabulary		
anclar (ᶜfondear) drop anchor (v)	**el dique seco** dry dock	**embarcar** board (v)
el guardacostas m **la guardacostas** f coast guard	**amarrar** moor (v)	**desembarcar** disembark (v)
el capitán del puerto m **la capitana del puerto** f harbor master	**atracar** dock (v)	**zarpar** set sail (v)

los deportes
sports

el fútbol americano • football

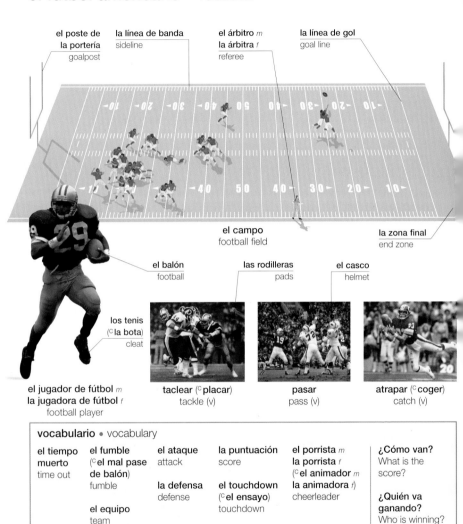

el poste de la portería
goalpost

la línea de banda
sideline

el árbitro *m*
la árbitra *f*
referee

la línea de gol
goal line

el campo
football field

la zona final
end zone

el balón
football

las rodilleras
pads

el casco
helmet

los tenis
(ᶜ la bota)
cleat

el jugador de fútbol *m*
la jugadora de fútbol *f*
football player

taclear (ᶜ placar)
tackle (v)

pasar
pass (v)

atrapar (ᶜ coger)
catch (v)

---

vocabulario • vocabulary

el tiempo muerto	el fumble	el ataque	la puntuación	el porrista *m*	¿Cómo van?
time out	(ᶜ el mal pase de balón)	attack	score	la porrista *f*	What is the score?
	fumble	la defensa	el touchdown	(ᶜ el animador *m*	
	el equipo	defense	(ᶜ el ensayo)	la animadora *f*)	¿Quién va ganando?
	team		touchdown	cheerleader	Who is winning?

el rugby • rugby

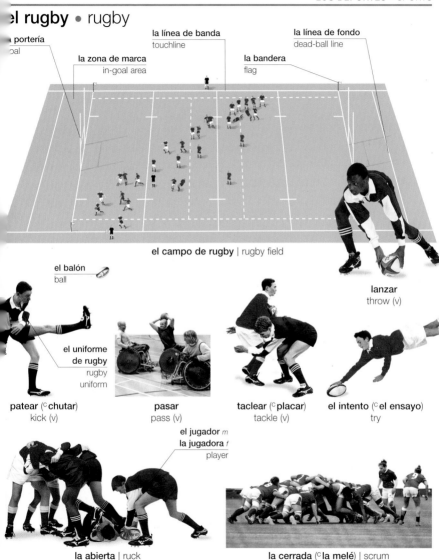

la portería
goal

la línea de banda
touchline

la línea de fondo
dead-ball line

la zona de marca
in-goal area

la bandera
flag

el campo de rugby | rugby field

el balón
ball

lanzar
throw (v)

el uniforme
de rugby
rugby
uniform

patear (ᶜchutar)
kick (v)

pasar
pass (v)

taclear (ᶜplacar)
tackle (v)

el intento (ᶜel ensayo)
try

el jugador m
la jugadora f
player

la abierta | ruck

la cerrada (ᶜla melé) | scrum

el fútbol • soccer

el balón
soccer ball

el delantero *m*
la delantera *f*
forward

el árbitro *m*
la árbitra *f*
referee

el círculo central
center circle

el portero *m*
la portera *f*
goalkeeper

el uniforme
soccer uniform

el futbolista *m*
la futbolista *f*
soccer player

el campo de fútbol
soccer field

el poste
goalpost

la red
net

el larguero
crossbar

regatear | dribble (v)

cabecear (ᶜtirar de cabeza) | head (v)

la barrera
wall

el gol | goal

tirar una falta | free kick

el área de penalti
penalty area

la línea de meta
goal line

el área de meta
goal area

la portería
goal

el defensa *m*
la defensa *f*
defender

el juez de línea *m*
la jueza de línea *f*
linesman

la bandera de esquina
corner flag

el saque de banda
throw-in

patear (ᶜ**chutar**)
kick (v)

los tacos (ᶜla bota)
cleat

mandar (ᶜ**hacer**) **un pase**
pass (v)

tirar
shoot (v)

hacer una entrada
tackle (v)

parar (ᶜ**hacer una parada**)
save (v)

vocabulario • vocabulary

el estadio stadium	**la tarjeta amarilla** yellow card	**la falta** foul	**la liga** league	**el cambio** substitution
marcar un gol score a goal (v)	**la tarjeta roja** red card	**el fuera de juego** offside	**el empate** tie	**el reserva** *m* **la reserva** *f* substitute
el penalti penalty	**el tiro de esquina** (ᶜ**el córner**) corner	**la expulsión** send off	**el descanso** half-time	**el tiempo extra** (ᶜ**la prórroga**) extra time

el hockey • hockey

el hockey sobre hielo • ice hockey

la zona de defensa
defending zone

la línea de meta
goal line

la zona de ataque
attack zone

la zona neutral
neutral zone

el portero
la portera
goalkeeper

la portería
goal

el círculo
de face-off
face-off circle

el círculo central
center circle

el guante
glove

la hombrera
pad

el patín de
cuchilla
ice skate

la pista de hockey sobre hielo
ice hockey rink

el palo
stick

el disco
puck

el jugador de hockey sobre hielo *m*
la jugadora de hockey sobre hielo *f*
ice hockey player

el hockey sobre hierba
field hockey

el palo de hockey
hockey stick

la pelota
ball

patinar
skate (v)

golpear
hit (v)

el críquet • cricket

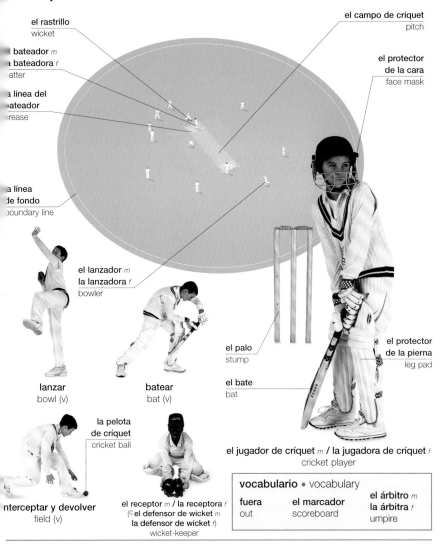

el rastrillo
wicket

el campo de críquet
pitch

el bateador *m*
la bateadora *f*
batter

el protector
de la cara
face mask

la línea del
bateador
crease

la línea
de fondo
boundary line

el lanzador *m*
la lanzadora *f*
bowler

el palo
stump

el protector
de la pierna
leg pad

el bate
bat

lanzar
bowl (v)

batear
bat (v)

interceptar y devolver
field (v)

la pelota
de críquet
cricket ball

el jugador de críquet *m* / la jugadora de críquet *f*
cricket player

el receptor *m* / la receptora *f*
(℃ el defensor de wicket *m*
la defensor de wicket *f*)
wicket-keeper

vocabulario • vocabulary		
fuera out	**el marcador** scoreboard	**el árbitro** *m* **la árbitra** *f* umpire

el baloncesto • basketball

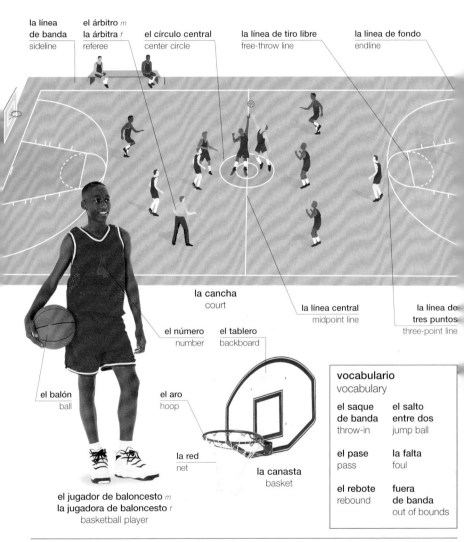

la línea de banda
sideline

el árbitro *m*
la árbitra *f*
referee

el círculo central
center circle

la línea de tiro libre
free-throw line

la línea de fondo
endline

la cancha
court

la línea central
midpoint line

la línea de tres puntos
three-point line

el número
number

el tablero
backboard

el balón
ball

el aro
hoop

la red
net

la canasta
basket

el jugador de baloncesto *m*
la jugadora de baloncesto *f*
basketball player

vocabulario
vocabulary

el saque de banda throw-in	**el salto entre dos** jump ball
el pase pass	**la falta** foul
el rebote rebound	**fuera de banda** out of bounds

as acciones • actions

lanzar
throw (v)

cachar (ᶜ **coger**)
catch (v)

tirar
shoot (v)

saltar
jump (v)

marcar
mark (v)

bloquear
block (v)

botar
dribble (v)

hacer canasta
(ᶜ **hacer un mate**)
dunk (v)

el vóleibol • volleyball

bloquear
block (v)

la red
net

recibir
dig (v)

el árbitro *m*
la árbitra *f*
referee

la rodillera
knee support

la cancha | court

el béisbol • baseball

el campo • field

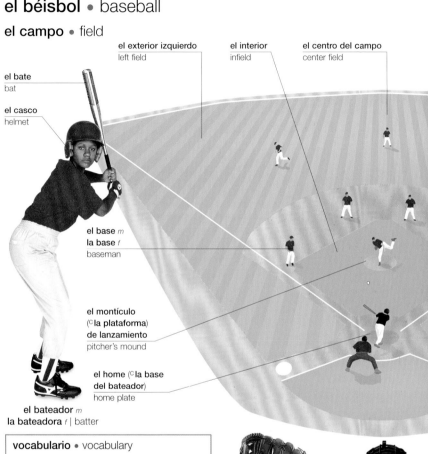

el exterior izquierdo
left field

el interior
infield

el centro del campo
center field

el bate
bat

el casco
helmet

el base *m*
la base *f*
baseman

el montículo
(^Cla plataforma)
de lanzamiento
pitcher's mound

el home (^Cla base
del bateador)
home plate

el bateador *m*
la bateadora *f* | batter

---

vocabulario • vocabulary

el turno inning	safe (^Ca salvo) safe	el strike strike
la carrera run	fuera out	el foul (^Cel fallo) foul ball

la bola
(^Cla pelota)
ball

la manopla (^Cel guante)
glove

la careta (^Cla máscara)
mask

español • english

el exterior
outfield

el exterior derecho
right field

la línea
de falta
foul line

el equipo
team

la banca
(ᶜel banquillo)
dugout

el catcher *m*
la catcher *f*
catcher

el lanzador *m*
la lanzadora *f*
pitcher

las acciones • actions

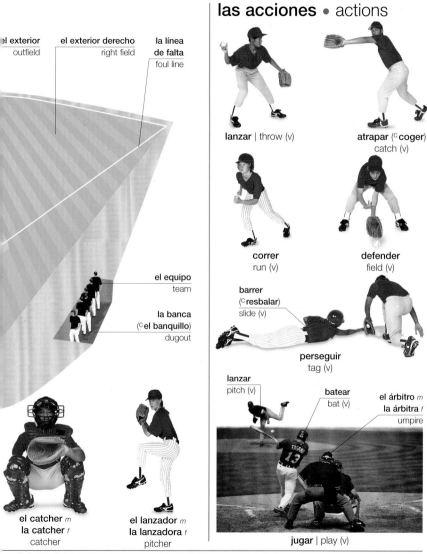

lanzar | throw (v)

atrapar (ᶜ**coger**)
catch (v)

correr
run (v)

defender
field (v)

barrer
(ᶜresbalar)
slide (v)

perseguir
tag (v)

lanzar
pitch (v)

batear
bat (v)

el árbitro *m*
la árbitra *f*
umpire

FASANO
13

jugar | play (v)

el tenis • tennis

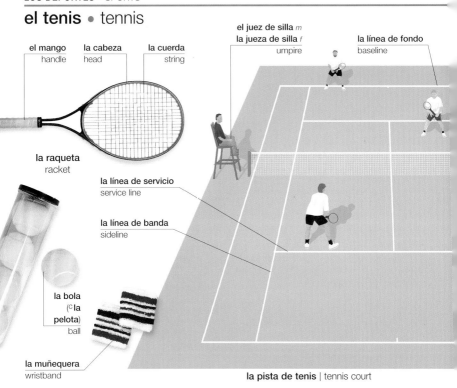

el mango
handle

la cabeza
head

la cuerda
string

la raqueta
racket

el juez de silla *m*
la jueza de silla *f*
umpire

la línea de fondo
baseline

la línea de servicio
service line

la línea de banda
sideline

la bola
(^Cla pelota)
ball

la muñequera
wristband

la pista de tenis | tennis court

---

vocabulario • vocabulary

el juego game	**el set** set	**nada** love	**la falta** fault	**el peloteo** rally	**el efecto** spin
los dobles doubles	**el partido** match	**la ventaja** advantage	**el as** ace	**¡red!** let!	**el juez de línea** *m* **la jueza de línea** *f* linesman
el singles (^C**el individual**) singles	**el tiebreak** tiebreaker	**cuarenta iguales** deuce	**la dejada** drop shot	**el tiro con efecto** slice	**el campeonato** championship

la red
net

el remate (ᶜ el mate)
smash

el recogepelotas *m*
la recogepelotas *f*
ball boy / ball girl

sacar
serve (v)

los tenis
tennis shoes

el jugador *m* / la jugadora *f*
player

los golpes • strokes

el servicio
serve

la volea
volley

el resto
return

el globo
lob

el derecho
forehand

el revés
backhand

los juegos de raqueta • racket games

el gallo
(ᶜ el volante)
shuttlecock

la raqueta
(ᶜ la pala)
paddle

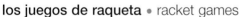

el bádminton
badminton

el ping-pong
table tennis

el squash
squash

el racketball
racquetball

el golf • golf

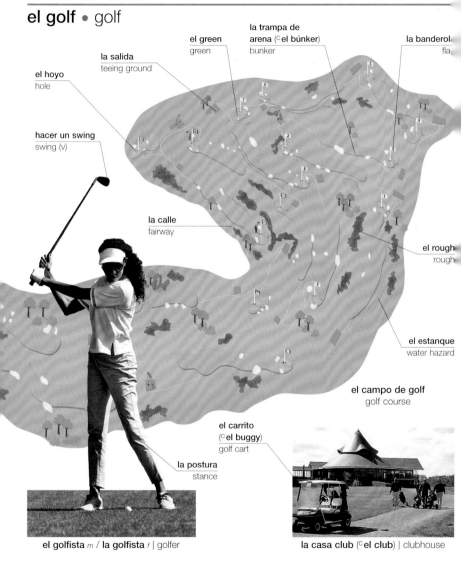

el green
green

la trampa de
arena (C el búnker)
bunker

la banderol
fla

la salida
teeing ground

el hoyo
hole

hacer un swing
swing (v)

la calle
fairway

el rough
rough

el estanque
water hazard

el campo de golf
golf course

el carrito
(C el buggy)
golf cart

la postura
stance

el golfista m / la golfista f | golfer

la casa club (C el club) | clubhouse

el equipo • equipment

los palos de golf
golf clubs

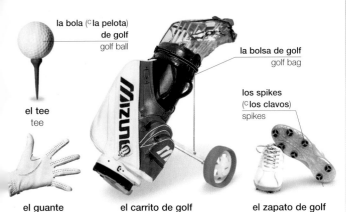

la bola (^Cla pelota) de golf
golf ball

la bolsa de golf
golf bag

los spikes
(^Clos clavos)
spikes

el tee
tee

el guante
glove

el carrito de golf
bag cart

el zapato de golf
golf shoe

la madera
wood

el putter
putter

el hierro (^Cel palo de hierro)
iron

el wedge
wedge

las acciones • actions

salir
tee off (v)

hacer un drive
drive (v)

tirar al hoyo con un putter
putt (v)

hacer un chip
chip (v)

vocabulario • vocabulary

el par par	**el sobre par** over par	**el hándicap** handicap	**el caddy** caddy	**el golpe** stroke	**el backswing** backswing
el bajo par under par	**el hoyo en uno** hole in one	**el torneo** tournament	**los espectadores** *m* **las espectadores** *f* spectators	**el swing de práctica** practice swing	**la línea de juego** line of play

el atletismo • track and field

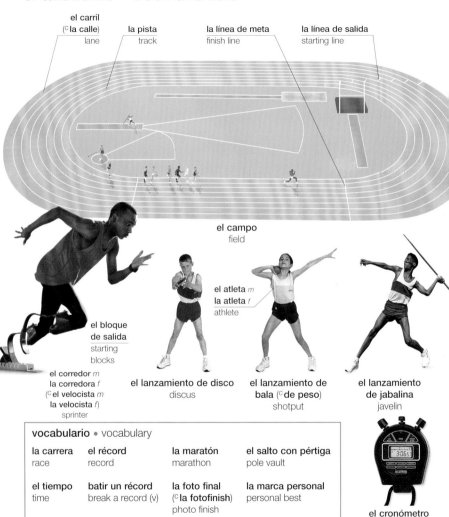

el carril
(ᶜla calle)
lane

la pista
track

la línea de meta
finish line

la línea de salida
starting line

el campo
field

el atleta m
la atleta f
athlete

el bloque
de salida
starting
blocks

el corredor m
la corredora f
(ᶜel velocista m
la velocista f)
sprinter

el lanzamiento de disco
discus

el lanzamiento de
bala (ᶜde peso)
shotput

el lanzamiento
de jabalina
javelin

vocabulario • vocabulary

la carrera	el récord	la maratón	el salto con pértiga
race	record	marathon	pole vault

el tiempo	batir un récord	la foto final	la marca personal
time	break a record (v)	(ᶜla fotofinish)	personal best
		photo finish	

el cronómetro
stopwatch

el relevo
(°el testigo)
baton

la carrera de relevos
relay race

la barra
(°el listón)
crossbar

el salto de altura
high jump

el salto de longitud
long jump

la carrera de vallas
hurdles

la gimnasia • gymnastics

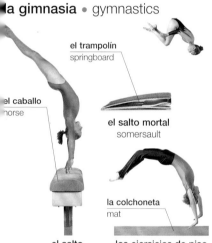

el trampolín
springboard

el gimnasta m
la gimnasta f
gymnast

el caballo
horse

el salto mortal
somersault

la viga (°la barra) de equilibrio
balance beam

el listón
(°la cinta)
ribbon

la colchoneta
mat

el salto
vault

los ejercicios de piso
(°de suelo)
floor exercises

la voltereta
cartwheel

la gimnasia rítmica
rhythmic gymnastics

---

vocabulario • vocabulary

las barras paralelas (°**las paralelas**) parallel bars	**las barras** (°**las paralelas**) **asimétricas** asymmetric bars	**las argollas** (°**las anillas**) rings	**las medallas** medals	**la plata** silver
la barra fija horizontal bar	**el caballo con arcos** pommel horse	**el podio** podium	**el oro** gold	**el bronce** bronze

los deportes de combate • combat sports

el contrincante *m*
la contrincante *f*
opponent

el protector
guard

el guante
glove

el cinturón
belt

el karate
karate

el taekwondo
tae kwon do

la careta
mask

el judo
judo

la espada
sword

el aikido
aikido

el kendo
kendo

el kung fu
kung fu

el full contact
kickboxing

la lucha libre
wrestling

el boxeo
boxing

os movimientos • actions

la caída
fall

el agarre
hold

el derribo
throw

la inmovilización
pin

la patada
kick

el puñetazo
punch

el golpe
strike

el salto
jump

el bloqueo (ᶜ **la parada**)
block

el golpe
chop

---

vocabulario • vocabulary

el ring boxing ring	**el combate** bout	**el puño** fist	**el cinturón negro** black belt	**la capoeira** capoeira
los guantes de boxeo boxing gloves	**el round** (ᶜ **el asalto**) round	**el nocaut** (ᶜ **el K.O.**) knockout	**la defensa personal** self-defense	**el sumo** sumo wrestling
el protegedientes mouth guard	**el entrenamiento** sparring	**el saco de arena** punching bag	**las artes marciales** martial arts	**el tai-chi** tai chi

la natación • swimming

el equipo • equipment

los flotadores
(ᶜ **los manguitos**)
water wings

los goggles (ᶜ **las gafas**
de natación)
goggles

la pinza
para la nariz
nose clip

la tabla (ᶜ **el flotador**)
kickboard

el traje de baño
swimsuit

la gorra (ᶜ **el**
gorro de baño)
swimming cap

el carril
(ᶜ **la calle**)
lane

el agua
water

el bloque de
salida
starting block

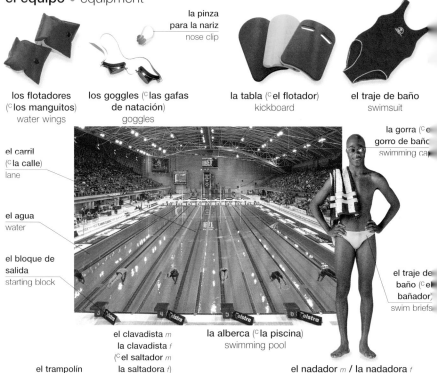

el traje de
baño (ᶜ **el**
bañador)
swim briefs

el clavadista *m*
la clavadista *f*
(ᶜ **el saltador** *m*
la saltadora *f*)
diver

la alberca (ᶜ **la piscina**)
swimming pool

el trampolín
diving board

el nadador *m* / **la nadadora** *f*
swimmer

tirarse un clavado (ᶜ **tirarse**
de cabeza) | dive (v)

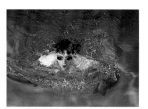

nadar | swim (v)

el giro | turn

os estilos • styles

el crol
front crawl

el pecho (ᶜ**la braza**)
breaststroke

la brazada
stroke

la patada
kick

el dorso (ᶜ**la espalda**) | backstroke

la mariposa | butterfly

el buceo • scuba diving

el tanque (ᶜla
botella de aire)
air tank

el visor
(ᶜlas gafas
de bucear)
mask

el regulador
regulator

el tubo
snorkel

el traje de buzo
wetsuit

la aleta
fin

el cinturón
de pesas
weight belt

---

vocabulario • vocabulary

el clavado (ᶜ**el salto**) dive	**hacer agua** tread water (v)	**el clavado** (ᶜ**el salto**) **de salida** racing dive	**la zona profunda** deep end	**el calambre** cramp	**el nado sincronizado** (ᶜ**la natación sincronizado**) synchronized swimming
el clavado (ᶜ**el salto**) **alto** high dive	**las taquillas** lockers **el waterpolo** water polo	**el salvavidas** m **la salvavidas** f (ᶜ**el socorrista** m **la socorrista** f) lifeguard	**la zona poco profunda** shallow end	**ahogarse** drown (v)	

la vela • sailing

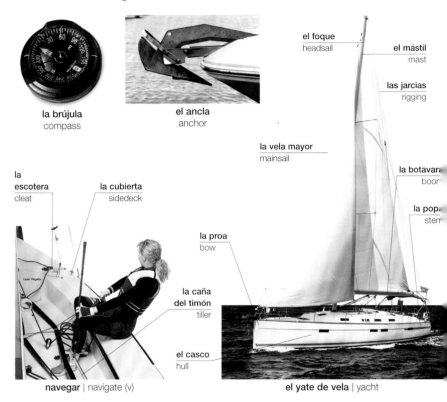

la brújula
compass

el ancla
anchor

el foque
headsail

el mástil
mast

las jarcias
rigging

la vela mayor
mainsail

la botavara
boom

la popa
stern

la escotera
cleat

la cubierta
sidedeck

la proa
bow

la caña del timón
tiller

el casco
hull

navegar | navigate (v)

el yate de vela | yacht

la seguridad • safety

la bengala
flare

el salvavidas
life buoy

el chaleco salvavidas
life jacket

la balsa salvavidas
life raft

los deportes acuáticos • watersports

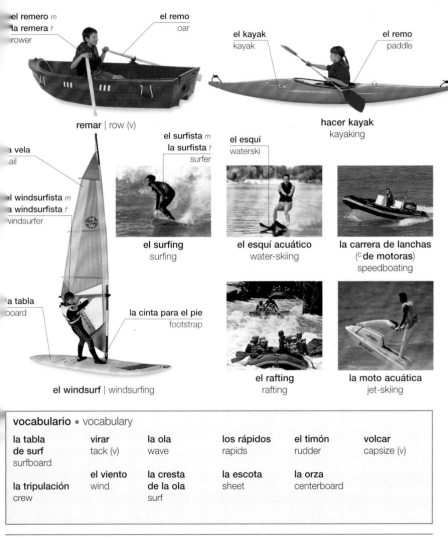

el remero *m*
la remera *f*
rower

el remo
oar

el kayak
kayak

el remo
paddle

remar | row (v)

hacer kayak
kayaking

la vela
sail

el windsurfista *m*
la windsurfista *f*
windsurfer

la tabla
board

el surfista *m*
la surfista *f*
surfer

el esquí
waterski

el surfing
surfing

el esquí acuático
water-skiing

la carrera de lanchas
(ᶜ **de motoras**)
speedboating

la cinta para el pie
footstrap

el windsurf | windsurfing

el rafting
rafting

la moto acuática
jet-skiing

---

vocabulario • vocabulary

la tabla de surf surfboard	**virar** tack (v)	**la ola** wave	**los rápidos** rapids	**el timón** rudder	**volcar** capsize (v)
la tripulación crew	**el viento** wind	**la cresta de la ola** surf	**la escota** sheet	**la orza** centerboard	

la equitación • horseback riding

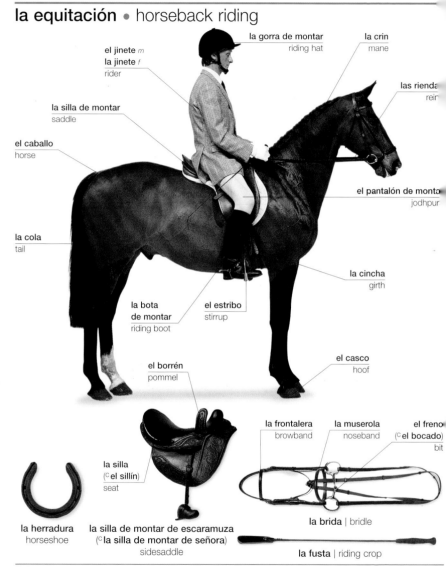

la gorra de montar
riding hat

la crin
mane

el jinete *m*
la jinete *f*
rider

las riendas
reins

la silla de montar
saddle

el caballo
horse

el pantalón de montar
jodhpur

la cola
tail

la cincha
girth

**la bota
de montar**
riding boot

el estribo
stirrup

el casco
hoof

el borrén
pommel

la silla
(ᶜ **el sillín**)
seat

la frontalera
browband

la muserola
noseband

el freno
(ᶜ **el bocado**)
bit

la herradura
horseshoe

la silla de montar de escaramuza
(ᶜ **la silla de montar de señora**)
sidesaddle

la brida | bridle

la fusta | riding crop

as modalidades • events

el caballo de carreras
racehorse

la valla
fence

la carrera de caballos
horse race

la carrera de obstáculos
steeplechase

la carrera al trote
harness race

el rodeo
rodeo

el concurso de saltos
show jumping

la carrera de carrozas
carriage race

el paseo
trail riding

la doma y monta
dressage

el polo
polo

---

vocabulario • vocabulary

el paso walk	**el medio galope** canter	**el salto** jump	**el cabestro** halter	**el cercado** paddock	**el hipódromo** racecourse
el trote trot	**el galope** gallop	**el mozo de cuadra** groom	**la cuadra** stable	**el ruedo** arena	**la carrera sin obstáculos** flat race

---

la pesca • fishing

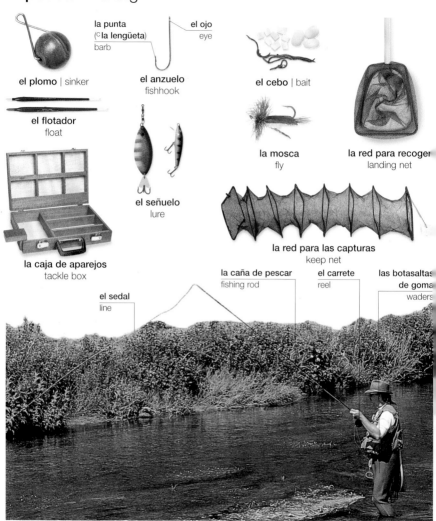

el plomo | sinker

la punta
(^Cla lengüeta)
barb

el ojo
eye

el anzuelo
fishhook

el cebo | bait

la mosca
fly

la red para recoger
landing net

el flotador
float

el señuelo
lure

la red para las capturas
keep net

la caja de aparejos
tackle box

la caña de pescar
fishing rod

el carrete
reel

**las botasaltas
de goma**
waders

el sedal
line

el pescador de caña *m* / **la pescadora de caña** *f* | angler

os tipos de pesca • types of fishing

la pesca en agua dulce
freshwater fishing

la pesca con mosca
fly-fishing

la pesca deportiva
sportfishing

la pesca de altura
deep-sea fishing

la pesca en la orilla
surfcasting

las acciones • activities

lanzar
cast (v)

atrapar (ᶜcoger)
catch (v)

recoger
reel in (v)

atrapar (ᶜcoger)
con la red
net (v)

soltar
release (v)

---

vocabulario • vocabulary

cebar bait (v)	**los aparejos** tackle	**la ropa impermeable** rain gear	**la licencia de pesca** fishing license	**la nasa** creel
picar bite (v)	**el carrete** spool	**la pértiga** pole	**la pesca en alta mar** marine fishing	**la pesca con arpón** spearfishing

español • english

el esquí • skiing

la pista
ski slope

la telesilla
chairlift

la góndola
(ᶜ el teleférico)
cable car

la pista de esquí
ski run

el guante
glove

el bastón
ski pole

la barrera
de seguridad
safety barrier

la punta
tip

el canto
edge

el esquí
ski

la chaqueta
de esquí
ski jacket

el esquiador m
la esquiadora f
skier

la bota de esquí
ski boot

as modalidades • events

el descenso
downhill skiing

el poste
gate

el slalom
slalom

el salto
ski jump

el esquí de fondo
cross-country skiing

los deportes de invierno • winter sports

la escalada en hielo
ice climbing

**el patinaje
sobre hielo**
ice-skating

los goggles
(ᶜlas gafas
de ventisca)
goggles

el patín
skate

el patinaje artístico
figure skating

el snowboarding
snowboarding

el bobsleigh
bobsled

el luge
luge

la moto de nieve
snowmobile

tirarse en trineo
sledding

---

vocabulario • vocabulary

el esquí alpino alpine skiing	**el curling** curling
el slalom gigante giant slalom	**el biatlón** biathlon
fuera de pista off-piste	**la avalancha** avalanche
el trineo con perros dogsledding	**el patinaje de velocidad** speed skating

---

los otros deportes • other sports

el planeador
glider

el ala delta
hang-glider

el vuelo sin motor
gliding

el paracaídas
parachute

el vuelo con ala delta
hang-gliding

la cuerda
rope

la escalada
rock climbing

el paracaidismo
parachuting

el parapente
paragliding

el paracaidismo en caída libre
skydiving

el rappel
rappelling

el salto bungee (ᶜel puenting)
bungee jumping

el piloto de carreras *m*
la piloto de carreras *f*
race-car driver

el rally
rally driving

el automovilismo
auto racing

el motocross
motocross

el motociclismo
motorcycle racing

la patineta
(^c el monopatín)
skateboard

el palo
stick

la
máscara
mask

el florete
foil

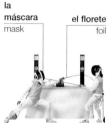

andar en patineta
^c montar en monopatín)
skateboarding

el patinaje en línea
inline skating

el lacrosse
lacrosse

el esgrima
fencing

el pino (^c el bolo)
pin

la flecha
arrow

el carcaj
quiver

el arco
bow

la diana
target

el tiro con arco
archery

el tiro
target shooting

la bola
de boliche
(^c de bowling)
bowling ball

el boliche (^c los bolos)
bowling

el pool (^c el billar
americano) | pool

el billar
snooker

la forma física • fitness

la bicicleta fija
exercise bike

la máquina de ejercicios
gym machine

el banco
bench

las pesas
free weights

la barra
bar

el gimnasio
gym

la máquina
de remos
rowing machine

la caminadora (ᶜla
banda de paseo)
treadmill

la máquina
de cross
elliptical trainer

el entrenador personal *m*
la entrenadora personal *f*
personal trainer

la máquina
de step
stair machine

la alberca
(ᶜla piscina)
swimming pool

el sauna (ᶜla sauna)
sauna

os ejercicios • exercises

el estiramiento
stretch

la flexión con
estiramiento
lunge

la flexión
push-up

la pesa
dumbbell

ponerse en cuclillas
squat

el abdominal
sit-up

el ejercicio
de bíceps
bicep curl

los ejercicios de piernas
leg press

los ejercicios
pectorales
chest press

las
zapatillas
sneakers

el levantamiento
de pesas
weight training

la barra
de pesas
weight bar

el jogging
(ᶜ el footing)
jogging

el pilates
Pilates

---

vocabulario • vocabulary

entrenar train (v)	correr en parada jog in place (v)	estirar extend (v)	la gimnasia prepugilística boxercise	saltar a la comba jumping rope
calentar warm up (v)	flexionar flex (v)	levantar pull up (v)	el entrenamiento en circuito circuit training	la clase de spinning spin class

---

el ocio
leisure

el teatro • theater

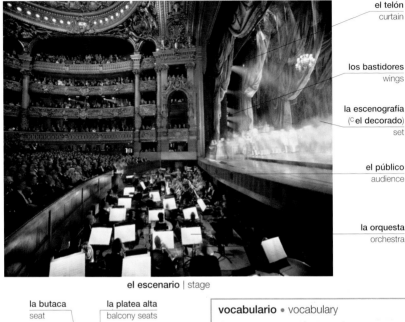

el telón
curtain

los bastidores
wings

la escenografía
(c el decorado)
set

el público
audience

la orquesta
orchestra

el escenario | stage

la butaca
seat

la platea alta
balcony seats

la fila
row

el palco
box

la platea
mezzanine

la galería
balcony

el pasillo
aisle

las butacas
generales
(c el patio
de butacas)
orchestra
seats

las butacas | seating

vocabulario • vocabulary

la obra
de teatro
play

el productor m
la productora f
producer

el foso de
la orquesta
orchestra pit

el reparto
cast

el guión
script

el entreacto
(c el descanso)
intermission

el actor m
la actriz f
actor

el telón
de fondo
backdrop

el director m
la directora f
director

el estreno
opening night

el programa
program

el concierto
concert

el musical
musical

el vestuario
(ᶜ el traje)
costume

el ballet
ballet

vocabulario • vocabulary

el acomodador *m*
la acomodadora *f*
usher

la música clásica
classical music

la partitura
musical score

la banda sonora
soundtrack

aplaudir
applaud (v)

el bis
encore

Quisiera dos entradas para la sesión de esta noche.
I'd like two tickets for tonight's performance.

¿A qué hora empieza?
What time does it start?

la ópera
opera

el cine • movies

las
palomitas
popcorn

el cine
movie theater

el
póster
poster

la taquilla
box office

el vestíbulo
lobby

la pantalla
screen

vocabulario • vocabulary

la comedia
comedy

la película de suspense
thriller

la película de terror
horror movie

la película de vaqueros
(ᶜ del oeste)
Western

la película romántica
romance

la película de ciencia ficción
science fiction movie

la película de aventuras
adventure movie

la película de dibujos animados
animated movie

la orquesta • orchestra

la cuerda • strings

el arpa
harp

el director de orquesta *m*
la directora de orquesta *f*
conductor

el contraba,
double bas

el violín
violin

el podio
podium

la viola
viola

el violoncelo
cello

la partitura
score

la clave de sol
treble clef

la nota
note

el pentagrama
staff

la clave de fa
bass clef

el piano | piano

la notación | notation

---

vocabulario • vocabulary

la obertura	la sonata	la pausa	sostenido	el becuadro	la escala
overture	sonata	rest	sharp	natural	scale
la sinfonía	los instrumentos	el tono	bemol	el compás	la batuta
symphony	instruments	pitch	flat	bar	baton

---

viento-madera • woodwind

el flautín
piccolo

la flauta transversal
(ᶜ**la flauta travesera**)
flute

el oboe
oboe

el corno inglés
English horn

el clarinete
clarinet

el clarinete bajo
bass clarinet

el fagot
bassoon

el contrafagot
double bassoon

el saxofón
saxophone

la percusión • percussion

el vibráfono
vibraphone

los bongos
bongos

el tambor pequeño
snare drum

el timbal
kettledrum

el gong
gong

el triángulo
triangle

las maracas
maracas

los platillos
cymbals

el pandero
(ᶜ**la pandereta**)
tambourine

el pedal
foot pedal

el viento-metal • brass

la trompeta
trumpet

el trombón de varas
trombone

la trompa
French horn

la tuba
tuba

el concierto • concert

la bocina
(ᶜel altavoz)
speaker

los fans
fans

el vocalista *m*
la vocalista *f*
(ᶜel cantante *m*
la cantante *f*)
lead singer

el guitarrista *m*
la guitarrista *f*
guitarist

el micrófono
microphone

el batería *m*
la batería *f*
drummer

el concierto de rock | rock concert

los instrumentos • instruments

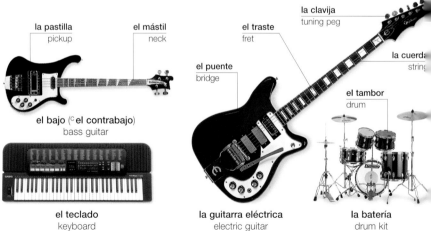

la pastilla
pickup

el mástil
neck

el bajo (ᶜel contrabajo)
bass guitar

el teclado
keyboard

el puente
bridge

el traste
fret

la clavija
tuning peg

la cuerda
string

el tambor
drum

la guitarra eléctrica
electric guitar

la batería
drum kit

s estilos musicales • musical styles

el jazz
jazz

el blues
blues

el góspel
gospel

la música folklórica (ᶜ folk)
folk music

el pop
pop

la música de baile
dance music

el rap
rap

el heavy metal
heavy metal

la música clásica
classical music

---

vocabulario • vocabulary

la canción	la letra	la melodía	el ritmo	el reggae	la música country	el reflector (ᶜ el foco)
song	lyrics	melody	beat	reggae	country	spotlight

el turismo • sightseeing

el turista *m*
la turista *f*
tourist

la atracción turística | tourist attraction

el itinerario
itinerary

descubierto
open-top

el autobús turístico | tour bus

el guía turístico *m*
la guía turística *f*
tour guide

la estatuilla
figurine

la visita guiada
(^Cla visita con guía)
guided tour

los recuerdos
souvenirs

vocabulario • vocabulary

el precio
de entrada
entrance fee

abierto *m*
abierta *f*
open

cerrado *m*
cerrada *f*
closed

la audioguía
audioguide

la guía
del viajero
guidebook

la cámara
(^Cla máquina)
fotográfica
camera

las pilas
batteries

el carrete
film

las
indicaciones
directions

la izquierda
left

la derecha
right

recto
straight ahead

¿Dónde está… ?
Where is… ?

Estoy perdido.
(^CMe he perdido.)
I'm lost.

¿Podría decirme
cómo se va a… ?
Can you tell me the
way to…?

os lugares de interés • attractions

el cuadro
painting

la muestra
exhibit

la estatua
statue

la exposición
exhibition

la ruina famosa
famous ruin

la galería de arte
art gallery

el monumento
monument

el museo
museum

**el edificio
histórico**
historic building

el casino
casino

los jardines
gardens

el parque nacional
national park

la información • information

las horas
times

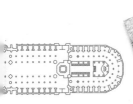

el plano de la planta
floor plan

el mapa (ᶜ el plano)
map

el horario
schedule

**la oficina de
información**
tourist information

las actividades al aire libre • outdoor activities

el sendero
footpath

el reloj de sol
sundial

la cafetería
café

el parque | park

el pasto
(ᶜla hierba)
grass

la banca
(ᶜel banco)
bench

los jardines
clásicos
formal gardens

la montaña rusa
roller coaster

la feria
fairground

el parque de diversiones
(ᶜel parque de atracciones)
theme park

el parque safari
(ᶜel safari park)
safari park

el zoológico
(ᶜel zoo)
zoo

las actividades • activities

el ciclismo
cycling

el jogging
jogging

la patineta
(ᶜ**montar en patinete**)
skateboarding

el patinaje
rollerblading

el sendero para caballos
bridle path

la canasta
(ᶜ**la cesta**)
picnic
basket

la ornitología
bird-watching

la equitación
horseback riding

la caminata
(ᶜ**el senderismo**)
hiking

el picnic
picnic

el área de juegos • playground

el cajón de arena
sandbox

la alberca (ᶜ**la piscina**)
de plástico
wading pool

los columpios
swing

el subibaja
seesaw

la resbaladilla (ᶜ**el tobogán**)
slide

el changuero
(ᶜ**la estructura para escalar**)
climbing frame

la playa • beach

el hotel
hotel

la sombrilla
beach umbrella

la arena
sand

la ola
wave

el ma
se

el asoleadero
sun lounger

el traje de baño
(ᶜ el bañador)
swimming briefs

la bolsa de playa
beach bag

el bikini
bikini

asolear (ᶜ**tomar el sol**) | sunbathe (v)

el salvavidas *m*
la salvavidas *f*
(^C el socorrista *m*
la socorrista *f*)
lifeguard

la torre de vigilancia
lifeguard tower

la barrera contra el viento
windbreak

el paseo marítimo
boardwalk

la silla de playa
(^C la hamaca)
deck chair

los lentes obscuros
(^C las gafas de sol)
sunglasses

el sombrero para el sol
sun hat

el bronceador
(^C la crema bronceadora)
suntan lotion

la crema protectora
sunscreen

el traje de baño
(^C el bañador)
swimsuit

la pelota de playa
beach ball

la llanta (^C el flotador)
inflatable ring

la pala
shovel

la cubeta
(^C el cubo)
pail

el castillo de arena
sandcastle

la toalla de playa
beach towel

la concha
shell

el camping • camping

el contenedor
de la basura
waste disposal

los baños
(ᶜlos aseos)
restrooms

las regaderas
(ᶜlas duchas)
shower block

el punto eléctrico
electric hookup

el toldo (ᶜel
doble techo)
rain fly

la estaca
(ᶜla clavija)
tent peg

el camping
campground

la cuerda
guy rope

la roulotte
camper

---

vocabulario • vocabulary

acampar
camp (v)

la oficina del director
site manager's office

**hay lugares (ᶜplazas)
libres**
sites available

lleno (ᶜcompleto)
full

el lugar (ᶜla plaza)
site

el catre de campaña
camp bed

**poner (ᶜmontar)
una tienda**
pitch a tent (v)

**el tubo (ᶜel palo)
de la tienda**
tent pole

la mesa de pícnic
picnic bench

la hamaca
hammock

el cámper
camper van

el remolque
trailer

el carbón vegetal
charcoal

la hoguera
campfire

**la pastilla para
fogatas (ᶜpara
hogueras)**
firelighter

**encender una
fogata (ᶜuna
hoguera)**
light a fire (v)

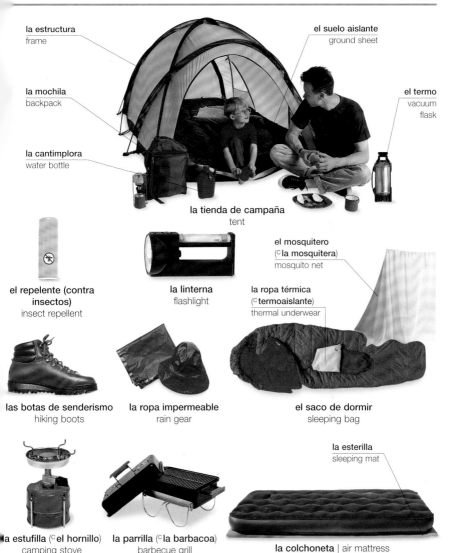

la estructura
frame

el suelo aislante
ground sheet

la mochila
backpack

el termo
vacuum flask

la cantimplora
water bottle

la tienda de campaña
tent

el repelente (contra insectos)
insect repellent

la linterna
flashlight

el mosquitero
(C la mosquitera)
mosquito net

la ropa térmica
(C termoaislante)
thermal underwear

las botas de senderismo
hiking boots

la ropa impermeable
rain gear

el saco de dormir
sleeping bag

la esterilla
sleeping mat

la estufilla (C el hornillo)
camping stove

la parrilla (C la barbacoa)
barbecue grill

la colchoneta | air mattress

la electronica de consumo • home entertainment

el televisor de pantalla plana
flatscreen TV

el amplificado
amplifie

la bocina
(^C el altavoz)
speaker

el pie de la bocina
(^C el pie del altavoz)
speaker stand

el avance rápido
fast-forward

el botón para
rebobinar
rewind

el play
play

la pausa
pause

el volumen
volume

el botón
para grabar
record

el stop
stop

el control remoto (^C el mando a distancia)
remote control

el reproductor de DVD
DVD player

el replicador de puerto
dock

el sintonizador digital
DTV converter box

la radio digital
digital radio

la antena parabólica
satellite dish

la consola
console

os controles
controller

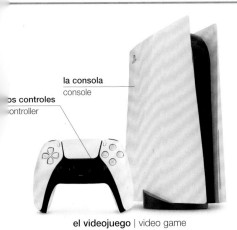

el videojuego | video game

el borde del ocular
eyecup

la pantalla
screen

la cámara de vídeo
camcorder

la bocina inteligente
smart speaker

el estuche
case

los audífonos inalámbricos
wireless earphones

la bocina bluetooth
(C **el altavoz bluetooth**)
bluetooth speaker

los audífonos
(C **los auriculares**)
headphones

vocabulario • vocabulary

el lector de discos compactos
CD player

la película
(C **el largometraje**)
feature film

el programa
program

digital
digital

el karaoke
karaoke

el estéreo
stereo

el anuncio
advertisement

alta definición
high-definition

el Wi-Fi
(C **la Wi-Fi**)
Wi-Fi

la televisión inteligente
smart TV

la transmisión por secuencias
streaming

la barra de sonido
soundbar

la televisión por cable
cable television

cambiar de canal
change channel (v)

encender la televisión
turn on the television (v)

apagar la televisión
turn off the television (v)

ver la televisión
watch television (v)

la fotografía • photography

el disparador
shutter release

el obturador
(ᶜla rueda del diafragma)
aperture dial

el lente
(ᶜel objetivo)
lens

la cámara réflex | SLR camera

el filtro
filter

la tapa del lente
(ᶜobjetivo)
lens cap

el flash electrónico
flash gun

el fotómetro
light meter

el zoom (ᶜel teleobjetivo)
zoom lens

el tripié (ᶜel trípode)
tripod

los tipos de cámara • types of camera

la cámara Polaroid
Polaroid camera

la cámara digital
digital camera

el flash
flash

el teléfono con cámara
camera phone

la cámara desechable
disposable camera

otografiar • photograph (v)

enfocar
focus (v)

revelar
develop (v)

el negativo
negative

el selfie
(ᶜla autofoto)
selfie

apaisado
andscape

en formato vertical
portrait

la fotografía | photograph

el álbum de fotos
photo album

el portarretratos
picture frame

los problemas • problems

subexpuesto
underexposed

sobreexpuesto
overexposed

desenfocado
out of focus

los ojos rojos
red eye

vocabulario • vocabulary

el visor viewfinder	**la copia** print
la funda de la cámara camera case	**mate** matte
la exposición exposure	**con brillo** gloss
la película film	**la ampliación** enlargement

Me gustaría revelar este rollo
(ᶜeste carrete).
I'd like this film processed.

los juegos • games

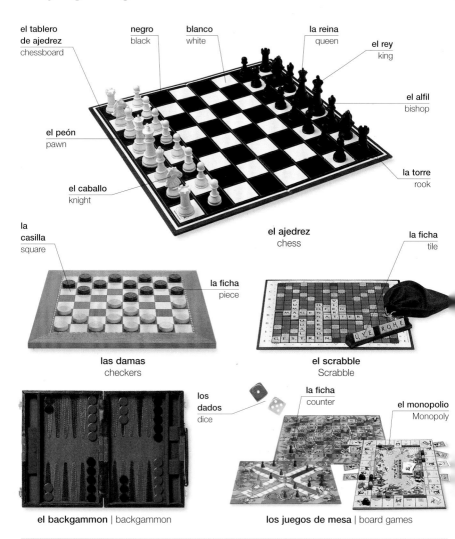

el tablero
de ajedrez
chessboard

negro
black

blanco
white

la reina
queen

el rey
king

el alfil
bishop

el peón
pawn

la torre
rook

el caballo
knight

la
casilla
square

el ajedrez
chess

la ficha
tile

la ficha
piece

las damas
checkers

el scrabble
Scrabble

los
dados
dice

la ficha
counter

el monopolio
Monopoly

el backgammon | backgammon

los juegos de mesa | board games

el rompecabezas (^C **el puzzle**)
jigsaw puzzle

el dominó
dominoes

la diana
dartboard

el blanco
(^C **el centro**)
bullseye

los dardos
darts

el comodín
joker

el joto (^C **la jota**)
jack

la reina
queen

el rey
king

el as
ace

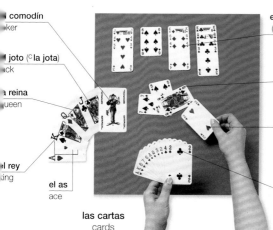

el diamante
(^C **el rombo**)
diamond

la espada
(^C **la pica**)
spade

el corazón
heart

el trébol
club

las cartas
cards

barajar | shuffle (v)

repartir (^C **dar**) | deal (v)

---

vocabulario • vocabulary

el turno move	**ganar** win (v)	**el perdedor** *m* **la perdedora** *f* loser	**el punto** point	**el bridge** bridge	**¿A quién** **le toca?** Whose turn is it?
jugar play (v)	**el ganador** *m* **la ganadora** *f* winner	**la partida** game	**la puntuación** score	**la baraja** deck of cards	**Te toca a ti.** It's your move.
el jugador *m* **la jugadora** *f* player	**perder** lose (v)	**la apuesta** bet	**el póquer** poker	**el palo** suit	**Tira los dados.** Roll the dice.

las manualidades • arts and crafts (1)

el artista *m*
la artista *f*
artist

el cuadro
painting

el caballete
easel

el lienzo
canvas

el pincel
brush

la paleta
palette

la pintura | painting

las pinturas
paints

la pintura al óleo
oil paint

las acuarelas
watercolor paint

los pasteles
pastels

la pintura acrílica
acrylic paint

la témpera
poster paint

los colores • colors

rojo
red

azul
blue

amarillo
yellow

verde
green

naranja
orange

morado
purple

blanco
white

negro
black

gris
gray

rosa
pink

marrón
brown

añil
indigo

as otras manualidades • other crafts

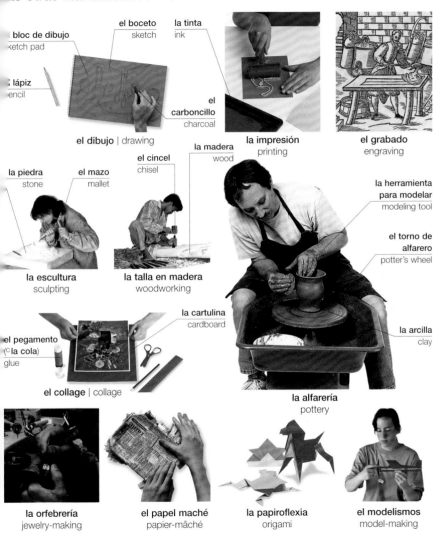

el bloc de dibujo
sketch pad

el lápiz
pencil

el boceto
sketch

la tinta
ink

el carboncillo
charcoal

el dibujo | drawing

la impresión
printing

el grabado
engraving

la piedra
stone

el mazo
mallet

el cincel
chisel

la madera
wood

la escultura
sculpting

la talla en madera
woodworking

la herramienta para modelar
modeling tool

el torno de alfarero
potter's wheel

la arcilla
clay

el pegamento
(° la cola)
glue

la cartulina
cardboard

el collage | collage

la alfarería
pottery

la orfebrería
jewelry-making

el papel maché
papier-mâché

la papiroflexia
origami

el modelismos
model-making

las manualidades • arts and crafts (2)

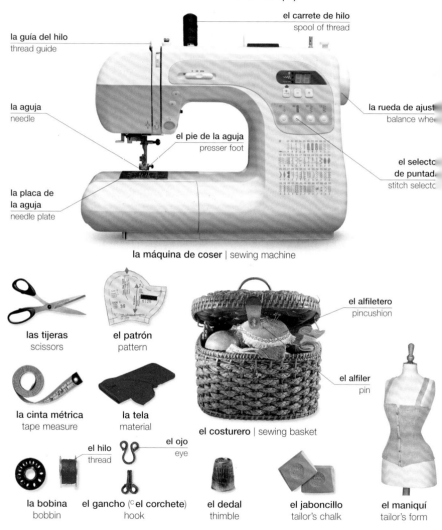

el carrete de hilo
spool of thread

la guía del hilo
thread guide

la aguja
needle

el pie de la aguja
presser foot

la rueda de ajust
balance whe

el selecto
de puntad
stitch selecto

la placa de
la aguja
needle plate

la máquina de coser | sewing machine

las tijeras
scissors

el patrón
pattern

el alfiletero
pincushion

el alfiler
pin

la cinta métrica
tape measure

la tela
material

el costurero | sewing basket

el hilo
thread

el ojo
eye

la bobina
bobbin

el gancho (ᶜ**el corchete**)
hook

el dedal
thimble

el jaboncillo
tailor's chalk

el maniquí
tailor's form

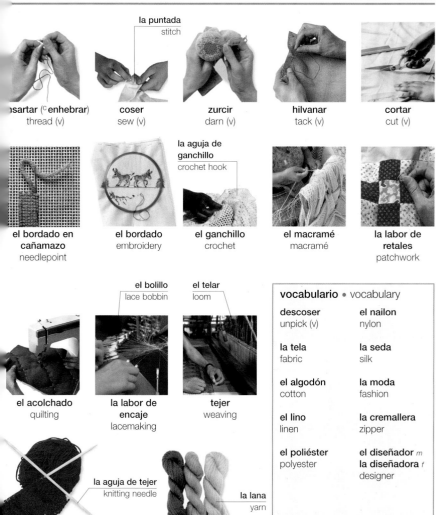

la puntada
stitch

sartar (^Cenhebrar)
thread (v)

coser
sew (v)

zurcir
darn (v)

hilvanar
tack (v)

cortar
cut (v)

el bordado en cañamazo
needlepoint

el bordado
embroidery

la aguja de ganchillo
crochet hook

el ganchillo
crochet

el macramé
macramé

la labor de retales
patchwork

el bolillo
lace bobbin

el telar
loom

el acolchado
quilting

la labor de encaje
lacemaking

tejer
weaving

la aguja de tejer
knitting needle

la labor de tejer | knitting

la lana
yarn

la madeja | skein

vocabulario • vocabulary	
descoser unpick (v)	**el nailon** nylon
la tela fabric	**la seda** silk
el algodón cotton	**la moda** fashion
el lino linen	**la cremallera** zipper
el poliéster polyester	**el diseñador** *m* **la diseñadora** *f* designer

el medio ambiente
environment

el espacio • space

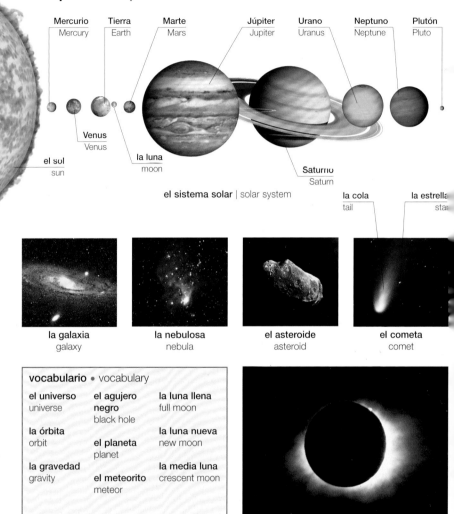

Mercurio
Mercury

Tierra
Earth

Marte
Mars

Júpiter
Jupiter

Urano
Uranus

Neptuno
Neptune

Plutón
Pluto

Venus
Venus

la luna
moon

el sol
sun

Saturno
Saturn

el sistema solar | solar system

la cola
tail

la estrella
star

la galaxia
galaxy

la nebulosa
nebula

el asteroide
asteroid

el cometa
comet

vocabulario • vocabulary

el universo universe	**el agujero negro** black hole	**la luna llena** full moon
la órbita orbit	**el planeta** planet	**la luna nueva** new moon
la gravedad gravity	**el meteorito** meteor	**la media luna** crescent moon

el eclipse | eclipse

a exploración espacial • space exploration

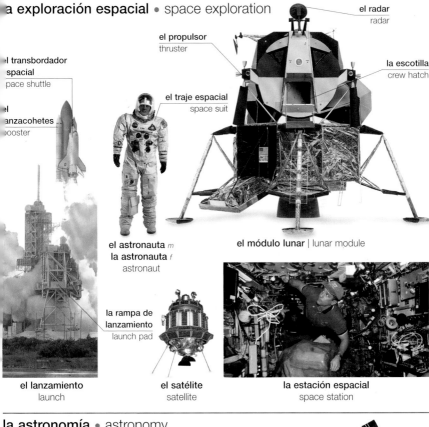

el radar
radar

el propulsor
thruster

l transbordador
spacial
pace shuttle

el
anzacohetes
booster

el traje espacial
space suit

la escotilla
crew hatch

el astronauta *m*
la astronauta *f*
astronaut

el módulo lunar | lunar module

la rampa de
lanzamiento
launch pad

el lanzamiento
launch

el satélite
satellite

la estación espacial
space station

la astronomía • astronomy

la constelación
constellation

los prismáticos
binoculars

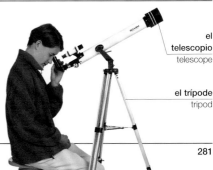

el
telescopio
telescope

el trípode
tripod

la Tierra • Earth

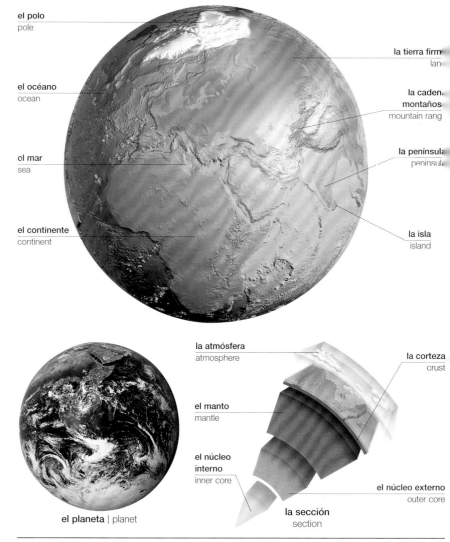

el polo
pole

el océano
ocean

el mar
sea

el continente
continent

la tierra firme
land

la cadena
montañosa
mountain range

la península
peninsula

la isla
island

la atmósfera
atmosphere

la corteza
crust

el manto
mantle

el núcleo
interno
inner core

el núcleo externo
outer core

el planeta | planet

la sección
section

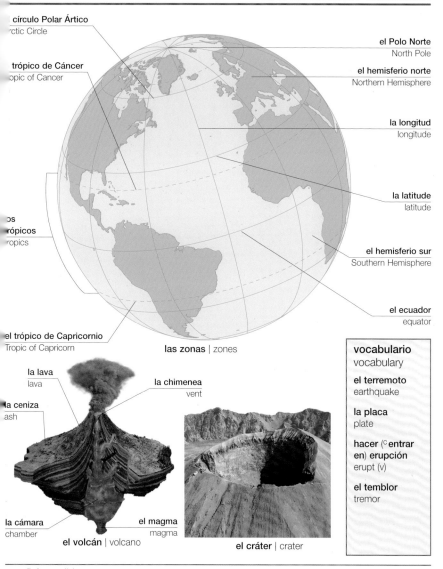

círculo Polar Ártico
rctic Circle

el Polo Norte
North Pole

trópico de Cáncer
opic of Cancer

el hemisferio norte
Northern Hemisphere

la longitud
longitude

la latitude
latitude

os
rópicos
ropics

el hemisferio sur
Southern Hemisphere

el ecuador
equator

el trópico de Capricornio
Tropic of Capricorn

las zonas | zones

la lava
lava

la chimenea
vent

la ceniza
ash

la cámara
chamber

el magma
magma

el volcán | volcano

el cráter | crater

vocabulario
vocabulary

el terremoto
earthquake

la placa
plate

hacer (ᶜ entrar en) erupción
erupt (v)

el temblor
tremor

el paisaje • landscape

la montaña
mountain

la ladera
slope

la orilla
bank

el río
river

los rápidos
rapids

las rocas
rocks

el glaciar
glacier

el valle | valley

la colina
hill

la meseta
plateau

el desfiladero
gorge

la cueva
cave

la llanura | plain

el desierto | desert

el bosque | forest

el bosque | woods

la selva tropical
rain forest

el pantano
swamp

el prado
meadow

la pradera
grassland

la cascada
waterfall

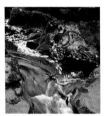
el arroyo
stream

el lago
lake

el géiser
geyser

la costa
coast

el acantilado
cliff

el arrecife de coral
coral reef

el estuario
estuary

el tiempo • weather

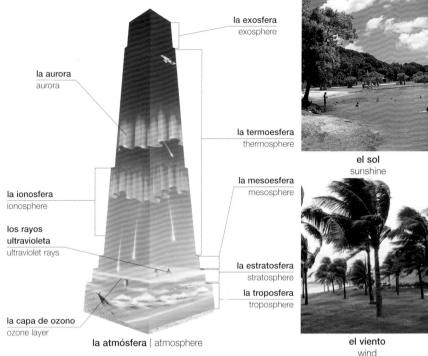

la exosfera
exosphere

la aurora
aurora

la termoesfera
thermosphere

el sol
sunshine

la mesoesfera
mesosphere

la ionosfera
ionosphere

los rayos
ultravioleta
ultraviolet rays

la estratosfera
stratosphere

la troposfera
troposphere

la capa de ozono
ozone layer

la atmósfera | atmosphere

el viento
wind

---

vocabulario • vocabulary

el aguanieve sleet	el chubasco shower	caluroso hot	seco dry	ventoso windy	**Tengo calor / frío.** I'm hot / cold.
el granizo hail	soleado sunny	frío cold	lluvioso wet	el temporal gale	**Está lloviendo.** It's raining.
el trueno thunder	nublado cloudy	cálido warm	húmedo humid	la temperatura temperature	**Estamos a… grados.** It's…degrees.

el relámpago
lightning

la nube
cloud

la lluvia
rain

la tormenta
storm

la neblina
mist

la niebla
fog

el arcoiris
rainbow

el carámbano
icicle

la nieve
snow

la escarcha
frost

el hielo
ice

la helada
freeze

el huracán
hurricane

el tornado
tornado

el monzón
monsoon

la inundación
flood

las rocas • rocks

ígneo • igneous

el granito
granite

la obsidiana
obsidian

el basalto
basalt

la piedra pómez
pumice

sedimentario • sedimentary

la piedra arenisca
sandstone

la piedra caliza
limestone

la tiza
chalk

el pedernal
flint

el conglomerado
conglomerate

el carbón
coal

metamórfico
metamorphic

la pizarra
slate

el esquisto
schist

el gneis
gneiss

el mármol
marble

las gemas • gems

el rubí
ruby

la amatista
amethyst

el azabache
jet

el ópalo
opal

la adularia
(ᶜla piedra lunar)
moonstone

el diamante
diamond

el granate
garnet

la aguamarina
aquamarine

el jade
jade

la esmeralda
emerald

el zafiro
sapphire

el topacio
topaz

la turmalina
tourmaline

os minerales • minerals

el cuarzo
quartz

la mica
mica

el azufre
sulfur

la hematita
(ᶜ**el hematites**)
hematite

la calcita
calcite

la malaquita
malachite

la turquesa
turquoise

el ónix (ᶜ**el ónice**)
onyx

el ágata
agate

el grafito
graphite

os metales • metals

el oro
gold

la plata
silver

el platino
platinum

el níquel
nickel

el hierro
iron

el cobre
copper

el estaño
tin

el aluminio
aluminum

el mercurio
mercury

el zinc
zinc

los animales • animals (1)

los mamíferos • mammals

los bigotes
whiskers

la cola
tail

el conejo
rabbit

el hámster
hamster

el ratón
mouse

la rata
rat

el erizo
hedgehog

la ardilla
squirrel

el murciélago
bat

el mapache
raccoon

el zorro
fox

el lobo
wolf

el cachorro
puppy

el gatito
kitten

la cría
pup

el perro
dog

el gato
cat

la nutria
otter

la foca
seal

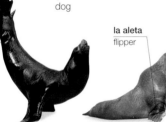

la aleta
flipper

el orificio nasal
blowhole

el león marino
sea lion

la morsa
walrus

la ballena
whale

el delfín
dolphin

la cornamenta
antler

la crin
mane

la joroba
(ᶜ la giba)
hump

la pezuña
hoof

el ciervo
deer

la cebra
zebra

la jirafa
giraffe

el camello
camel

la trompa
trunk

el colmillo
tusk

el cuerno
horn

el hipopótamo
hippopotamus

el elefante
elephant

el rinoceronte
rhinoceros

el tigre
tiger

la melena
lion's mane

el león
lion

el chango (ᶜ el mono)
monkey

el gorila
gorilla

el koala
koala

a bolsa
pouch

el oso panda
panda

la zarpa
claw

el canguro
kangaroo

el oso
bear

el oso polar
polar bear

los animales • animals (2)

las aves • birds

la cola
tail

el canario
canary

el gorrión
sparrow

el colibrí
hummingbird

la golondrina
swallow

la corneja
crow

la paloma
pigeon

el pájaro carpintero
woodpecker

el halcón
falcon

la lechuza
owl

la gaviota
gull

el águila
eagle

el pelícano
pelican

el flamenco
flamingo

la cigüeña
stork

la grulla
crane

el pingüino
penguin

el avestruz
ostrich

la oca | goose

el cisne
swan

el pavo real
peacock

el faisán
pheasant

el guajolote
(^{c}el pavo)
turkey

a cacatúa
cockatoo

el pico
beak

la pluma
feather

el ala
wing

la garra
claw

el loro
parrot

los reptiles • reptiles

las escamas
scales

el caimán
alligator

el lagarto
lizard

la iguana
iguana

el caparazón
shell

la tortuga
(^{c}el galápago)
turtle

la tortuga
tortoise

la serpiente
snake

el hocico
snout

el cocodrilo
crocodile

los animales • animals (3)

los anfibios • amphibians

la rana
frog

el sapo
toad

el renacuajo
tadpole

la salamandra
salamander

los peces • fish

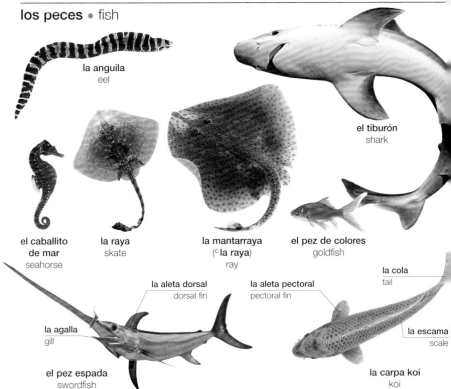

la anguila
eel

el tiburón
shark

**el caballito
de mar**
seahorse

la raya
skate

la mantarraya
(ᶜ **la raya**)
ray

el pez de colores
goldfish

la cola
tail

la aleta dorsal
dorsal fin

la aleta pectoral
pectoral fin

la agalla
gill

la escama
scale

el pez espada
swordfish

la carpa koi
koi

os invertebrados • invertebrates

la hormiga
ant

la termita
termite

la abeja
bee

la avispa
wasp

el escarabajo
beetle

la cucaracha
cockroach

la polilla
moth

la antena
antenna

la mariposa
butterfly

el capullo
cocoon

la oruga
caterpillar

el grillo
cricket

el saltamontes
grasshopper

la mantis
religiosa
praying mantis

el aquijón
sting

el alacrán
(ᶜ el escorpión)
scorpion

el ciempiés
centipede

la libélula
dragonfly

la mosca
fly

el mosquito
mosquito

la catarina
(ᶜ la mariquita)
ladybug

la araña
spider

la babosa
slug

el caracol
snail

el gusano
worm

la estrella de mar
starfish

el mejillón
mussel

el cangrejo
crab

la langosta
lobster

el pulpo
octopus

el calamar
squid

la medusa
jellyfish

las plantas • plants

el árbol • tree

la hoja
leaf

la ramita
twig

el sauce
willow

la rama
branch

la corteza
bark

el tronco
trunk

la raíz
root

el roble
oak

el álamo
poplar

el eucalipto
eucalyptus

el alerce
larch

la haya
beech

el abedul
birch

el pino
pine

el cedro
cedar

el arce
maple

el olmo
elm

el tilo
lime

el acebo
holly

la baya
berry

la palmera
palm

a planta de flor • flowering plant

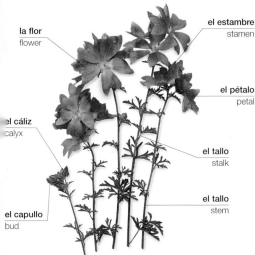

la flor
flower

el estambre
stamen

el pétalo
petal

el cáliz
calyx

el tallo
stalk

el tallo
stem

el capullo
bud

el ranúnculo
buttercup

la margarita
daisy

el cardo
thistle

el diente de león
dandelion

el brezo
heather

la amapola
poppy

la dedalera
foxglove

la madreselva
honeysuckle

el girasol
sunflower

el trébol
clover

los narcisos
silvestres
bluebells

la prímula
primrose

los lupinos
lupines

la ortiga
nettle

la ciudad • town

el callejón
alley

el edificio
de apartamentos
(C el edificio
de pisos)
apartment
building

la calle
street

la baliza
barrier

la plaza
square

la tienda
store

la esquina
street corner

el farol
(C la farola)
streetlight

el borde de
la banqueta
(C el bordillo)
curb

la banqueta
(C la acera)
sidewalk

el estacionamiento
(C el aparcamiento)
parking lot

la calle de
sentido único
one-way system

os edificios • buildings

el ayuntamiento
town hall

la biblioteca
library

el cine
movie theater

el teatro
theater

la universidad
university

el rascacielos
skyscraper

la escuela
school

las zonas • areas

la zona industrial
industrial park

el centro de la ciudad
downtown

el suburbio
(ᶜ **la periferia**)
suburb

el pueblo
village

---

vocabulario • vocabulary

la zona peatonal pedestrian zone	**la cuadra de oficinas** (ᶜ **el edificio de oficinas**) office block	**autobús** bus stop	**la fábrica** factory	**la alcantarilla** gutter	**el drenaje** (ᶜ **el sumidero**) drain
la avenida avenue		**la parada de la calle lateral** side street	**la coladera** (ᶜ **la boca de alcantarilla**) manhole	**la iglesia** church	

la arquitectura • architecture

los edificios y las estructuras • buildings and structures

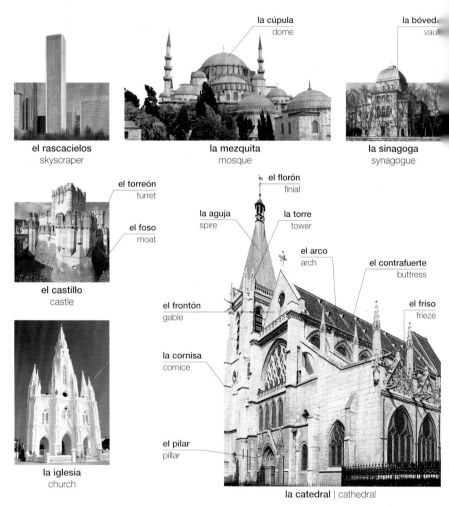

la cúpula
dome

la bóveda
vault

el rascacielos
skyscraper

la mezquita
mosque

la sinagoga
synagogue

el torreón
turret

el foso
moat

el castillo
castle

el florón
finial

la aguja
spire

la torre
tower

el arco
arch

el contrafuerte
buttress

el frontón
gable

el friso
frieze

la cornisa
cornice

el pilar
pillar

la iglesia
church

la catedral | cathedral

el templo
temple

el embalse
dam

el puente
bridge

los estilos • styles

el arquitrabe
architrave

el coro
choir

gótico
Gothic

renacentista
Renaissance

barroco
Baroque

rococó
Rococo

el frontón
pediment

neoclásico
Neoclassical

el estilo modernista
Art Nouveau

art decó
Art Deco

KING
FREDERICK
VIII
LAND

Glacial period ice,
average elevation
7,000 feet.

Etah

Qaanaaq
(Thule)

75°N

Petermann Pk. Danmarkshavn
9,646

Nuussuaq
(Kraulshavn)

BAFFIN
BAY

GREENLAND
(KALAALLIT
NUNAAT)
(Den.)

Ittoqqortoormiit
(Scoresbysund)

Upernavik

Clyde River
Uummannaq
qangiatugaapik

KING
CHRISTIAN IX
LAND

Jan
Mayen
(Nor.)

Arctic

Disko
Uummannaq

Qeqertarsuaq
(Godthavn)

Attu

Mt. Forel
11,024

Ísafjörður
Akureyri

Denmark Strait

FAEROE
(Den.)

Kangaamiut

Ammassalik

Ólafsvík
Reykjavík
ICELAND

Hekla

Surtsey
4,892

Shet

Nuuk
(Godthåb)

Paamiut
(Frederikshåb)

Tingmiarmiut

60°

Rockall

NORT

Alluitsup Paa
(Sydprøven)

Cape Farewell
(Nunap Isua)

Viking Longship
Leif Eriksson
1000 A.D.

NEWFOUNDLAND AND LABRADOR

Goose
Bay

NEWFOUNDLAND

St. John's

Cape
Breton I.

GRAND

NOVA SCOTIA

3,040

los datos
reference

el tiempo • time

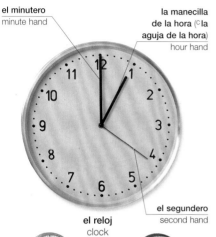

el minutero
minute hand

la manecilla
de la hora (ᶜla
aguja de la hora)
hour hand

el reloj
clock

el segundero
second hand

vocabulario • vocabulary

el segundo second	**ahora** now	**un cuarto de hora** a quarter of an hour
el minuto minute	**más tarde** later	**veinte minutos** twenty minutes
la hora hour	**media hora** half an hour	**cuarenta minutos** forty minutes

¿Qué hora es?
What time is it?

Son las tres en punto.
It's three o'clock.

la una y cinco
five past one

la una y diez
ten past one

la una y cuarto
quarter past one

la una y veinte
twenty past one

la una y veinticinco
twenty-five past one

la una y media
one thirty

**las veinticinco para
las dos** (ᶜlas dos
menos veinticinco)
twenty-five to two

las veinte para las dos
(ᶜlas dos menos veinte)
twenty to two

el cuarto para las dos
(ᶜlas dos menos cuarto)
quarter to two

las diez para las dos
(ᶜlas dos menos diez)
ten to two

las cinco para las dos
(ᶜlas dos menos cinco)
five to two

las dos en punto
two o'clock

a noche y el día • night and day

la medianoche
midnight

el amanecer
sunrise

el alba
dawn

la mañana
morning

el atardecer
(ᶜ**la puesta de sol**)
sunset

el mediodía
noon

el anochecer
dusk

la noche
evening

la tarde
afternoon

vocabulario • vocabulary

temprano early	**Llegas temprano.** You're early.	**Por favor, sé puntual.** Please be on time.	**¿A qué hora termina?** What time does it end?
puntual on time	**Llegas tarde.** You're late.	**Hasta luego.** I'll see you later.	**¿Cuánto dura?** How long will it last?
tarde late	**Llegaré dentro de poco.** I'll be there soon.	**¿A qué hora comienza?** What time does it start?	**Se está haciendo tarde.** It's getting late.

el calendario • calendar

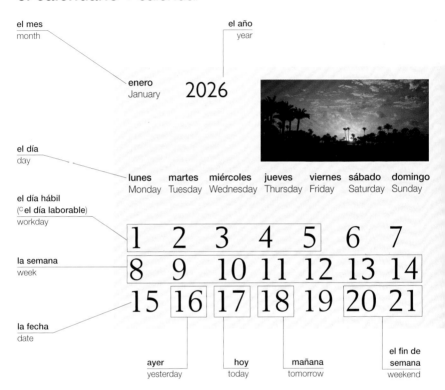

el mes
month

el año
year

enero
January

2026

el día
day

lunes | **martes** | **miércoles** | **jueves** | **viernes** | **sábado** | **domingo**
Monday | Tuesday | Wednesday | Thursday | Friday | Saturday | Sunday

el día hábil
(ᶜ el día laborable)
workday

la semana
week

la fecha
date

1	2	3	4	5	6	7
8	9	10	11	12	13	14
15	16	17	18	19	20	21

ayer
yesterday

hoy
today

mañana
tomorrow

el fin de
semana
weekend

---

vocabulario • vocabulary

| **enero** January | **marzo** March | **mayo** May | **julio** July | **septiembre** September | **noviembre** November |
| **febrero** February | **abril** April | **junio** June | **agosto** August | **octubre** October | **diciembre** December |

---

os años • years

1900	mil novecientos • nineteen hundred
1901	mil novecientos uno • nineteen oh one
1910	mil novecientos diez • nineteen ten
2000	dos mil • two thousand
2001	dos mil uno • two thousand and one

las estaciones • seasons

la primavera
spring

el verano
summer

el otoño
fall

el invierno
winter

vocabulario • vocabulary

el siglo
century

la década
decade

el milenio
millennium

quince días
two weeks

esta semana
this week

la semana pasada
last week

la semana que viene
next week

anteayer (°antes de ayer)
the day before yesterday

pasado mañana
the day after tomorrow

semanalmente
weekly

mensual
monthly

anual
annual

¿Qué día es hoy?
What's the date today?

Es el siete de febrero.
It's February seventh.

los números • numbers

0	cero • zero
1	uno • one
2	dos • two
3	tres • three
4	cuatro • four
5	cinco • five
6	seis • six
7	siete • seven
8	ocho • eight
9	nueve • nine
10	diez • ten
11	once • eleven
12	doce • twelve
13	trece • thirteen
14	catorce • fourteen
15	quince • fifteen
16	dieciséis • sixteen
17	diecisiete • seventeen
18	dieciocho • eighteen
19	diecinueve • nineteen

20	veinte • twenty
21	veintiuno • twenty-one
22	veintidós • twenty-two
30	treinta • thirty
40	cuarenta • forty
50	cincuenta • fifty
60	sesenta • sixty
70	setenta • seventy
80	ochenta • eighty
90	noventa • ninety
100	cien • one hundred
110	ciento diez • one hundred ten
200	doscientos • two hundred
300	trescientos • three hundred
400	cuatrocientos • four hundred
500	quinientos • five hundred
600	seiscientos • six hundred
700	setecientos • seven hundred
800	ochocientos • eight hundred
900	novecientos • nine hundred

1,000 · **mil** • one thousand

10,000 · **diez mil** • ten thousand

20,000 · **veinte mil** • twenty thousand

50,000 · **cincuenta mil** • fifty thousand

55,500 · **cincuenta y cinco mil quinientos** • fifty-five thousand five hundred

100,000 · **cien mil** • one hundred thousand

1,000,000 · **un millón** • one million

1,000,000,000 · **mil millones** • one billion

primero m **primera** f first	**segundo** m **segunda** f second	**tercero** m **tercera** f third

decimosexto m
decimosexta f
sixteenth

trigésimo m
trigésima f
thirtieth

decimoséptimo m
decimoséptima f
seventeenth

cuadragésimo m
cuadragésima f
fortieth

decimoctavo m
decimoctava f
eighteenth

quincuagésimo m
quincuagésima f
fiftieth

decimonoveno m
decimonovena f
nineteenth

sexagésimo m
sexagésima f
sixtieth

cuarto m **cuarta** f fourth	**octavo** m **octava** f eighth	**duodécimo** m **duodécima** f twelfth

vigésimo m
vigésima f
twentieth

septuagésimo m
septuagésima f
seventieth

quinto m **quinta** f fifth	**noveno** m **novena** f ninth	**decimotercero** m **decimotercera** f thirteenth

vigésimo primero m
vigésima primera f
twenty-first

octogésimo m
octogésima f
eightieth

sexto m **sexta** f sixth	**décimo** m **décima** f tenth	**decimocuarto** m **decimocuarta** f fourteenth

vigésimo segundo m
vigésima segunda f
twenty-second

nonagésimo m
nonagésima f
ninetieth

séptimo m **séptima** f seventh	**undécimo** m **undécima** f eleventh	**decimoquinto** m **decimoquinta** f fifteenth

vigésimo tercero m
vigésima tercera f
twenty-third

centésimo m
centésima f
(one) hundredth

los pesos y las medidas • weights and measures

el área • area

el pie cuadrado
square foot

el metro cuadrado
square meter

la distancia
distance

el kilómetro
kilometer

la milla
mile

la bandeja
pan

la libra
pound

la onza
ounce

el kilogramo
kilogram

el gramo
gram

la báscula (ᶜ **la balanza**) | scale

vocabulario • vocabulary

la yarda yard	**la tonelada** ton	**medir** measure (v)
el metro meter	**el miligramo** milligram	**pesar** weigh (v)

la longitud • length

el pie
foot

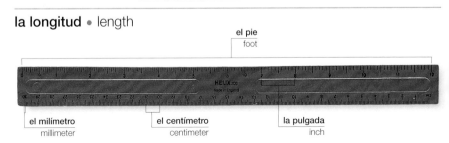

el milímetro
millimeter

el centímetro
centimeter

la pulgada
inch

español • english

la capacidad • capacity

el medio litro
half-liter

la pinta
pint

el volumen
volume

el mililitro
milliliter

la taza medidora (ᶜla jarra graduada)
measuring cup

la medida de capacidad
liquid measure

el recipiente • container

el tetrabrik
carton

el paquete
packet

la botella
bottle

la bolsa
bag

la tarrina | tub

el tarro | jar

la lata | tin

el pulverizador
spray bottle

la pastilla
bar

el tubo
tube

el rollo
roll

la lata
can

el spray
spray can

el mapamundi • world map

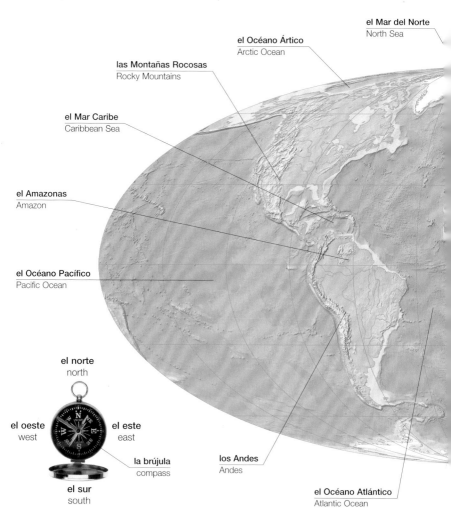

el Mar del Norte
North Sea

el Océano Ártico
Arctic Ocean

las Montañas Rocosas
Rocky Mountains

el Mar Caribe
Caribbean Sea

el Amazonas
Amazon

el Océano Pacífico
Pacific Ocean

el norte
north

el oeste
west

el este
east

la brújula
compass

el sur
south

los Andes
Andes

el Océano Atlántico
Atlantic Ocean

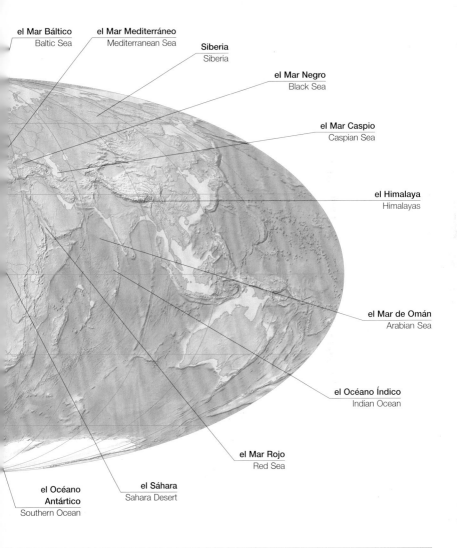

el Mar Báltico
Baltic Sea

el Mar Mediterráneo
Mediterranean Sea

Siberia
Siberia

el Mar Negro
Black Sea

el Mar Caspio
Caspian Sea

el Himalaya
Himalayas

el Mar de Omán
Arabian Sea

el Océano Índico
Indian Ocean

el Mar Rojo
Red Sea

el Océano
Antártico
Southern Ocean

el Sáhara
Sahara Desert

América del Norte y Central • North and Central America

Barbados • Barbados

Canadá • Canada

Costa Rica • Costa Rica

Cuba • Cuba

Jamaica • Jamaica

México • Mexico

Panamá • Panama

Trinidad y Tobago
Trinidad and Tobago

Estados Unidos de América
United States of America

Antigua y Barbuda
Antigua and Barbuda

Bahamas • Bahamas

Barbados • Barbados

Belice • Belize

Canadá • Canada

Costa Rica • Costa Rica

Cuba • Cuba

Dominica • Dominica

El Salvador • El Salvador

Estados Unidos de América
United States of America

Granada • Grenada

Groenlandia • Greenland

Guatemala • Guatemala

Haití • Haiti

Hawaii • Hawaii

Honduras • Honduras

Jamaica • Jamaica

México • Mexico

Nicaragua • Nicaragua

Panamá • Panama

Puerto Rico • Puerto Rico

República Dominicana
Dominican Republic

San Cristóbal y Nieves
St. Kitts and Nevis

San Vicente y las Granadinas
St. Vincent and the Grenadines

Santa Lucía • St. Lucia

Trinidad y Tobago
Trinidad and Tobago

América del Sur • South America

Argentina • Argentina

Bolivia • Bolivia

Brasil • Brazil

Chile • Chile

Colombia • Colombia

Ecuador • Ecuador

Perú • Peru

Uruguay • Uruguay

Venezuela • Venezuela

Argentina • Argentina

Bolivia • Bolivia

Brasil • Brazil

Chile • Chile

Colombia • Colombia

Ecuador • Ecuador

la Guayana Francesa
French Guiana

Guyana • Guyana

las Islas Galápagos
Galápagos Islands

las Malvinas • Falkland Islands

Paraguay • Paraguay

Perú • Peru

Surinam • Suriname

Uruguay • Uruguay

Venezuela • Venezuela

vocabulario • vocabulary

el continente
continent

el país
country

la nación
nation

el estado
state

el principado
principality

el territorio
territory

la colonia
colony

la zona
zone

la provincia
province

el distrito
district

la región
region

la capital
capital

Europa • Europe

Francia • France

Alemania • Germany

Italia • Italy

Polonia • Poland

Portugal • Portugal

España • Spain

Albania • Albania

Alemania • Germany

Andorra • Andorra

Austria • Austria

Belarús • Belarus

Bélgica • Belgium

Bosnia y Herzegovina
Bosnia and Herzegovina

Bulgaria • Bulgaria

Cerdeña • Sardinia

Ciudad del Vaticano
Vatican City

Córcega • Corsica

Chipre • Cyprus

Croacia • Croatia

Dinamarca • Denmark

Escocia • Scotland

Eslovaquia • Slovakia

Eslovenia • Slovenia

España • Spain

Estonia • Estonia

Federación Rusa
Russian Federation

Finlandia • Finland

Francia • France

Gales • Wales

Grecia • Greece

Hungría • Hungary

Inglaterra • England

Irlanda • Ireland

Irlanda del Norte
Northern Ireland

Islandia • Iceland

las Islas Baleares
Balearic Islands

Italia • Italy

Kaliningrado • Kaliningrad

Kosovo • Kosovo

Letonia • Latvia

Liechtenstein • Liechtenstein

Lituania • Lithuania

Luxemburgo • Luxembourg

Macedonia del Norte
North Macedonia

Malta • Malta

Moldavia • Moldova

Mónaco • Monaco

Montenegro • Montenegro

Noruega • Norway

Países Bajos • Netherlands

Polonia • Poland

Portugal • Portugal

Reino Unido • United Kingdom

República Checa
Czech Republic

Rumanía • Romania

San Marino • San Marino

Serbia • Serbia

Sicilia • Sicily

Suecia • Sweden

Suiza • Switzerland

Ucrania • Ukraine

África • Africa

gipto • Egypt

Etiopía • Ethiopia

Kenia • Kenya

Nigeria • Nigeria

Sudáfrica • South Africa

Uganda • Uganda

Angola • Angola
Argelia • Algeria
Benin • Benin
Botsuana • Botswana
Burquina Faso • Burkina Faso
Burundi • Burundi
Camerún • Cameroon
Chad • Chad
Comoros • Comoros
Congo • Congo
Costa de Marfil • Ivory Coast
Djibouti • Djibouti
Egipto • Egypt
Eritrea • Eritrea
Esuatini • Eswatini
Etiopía • Ethiopia
Gabón • Gabon
Gambia • Gambia
Ghana • Ghana
Guinea • Guinea
Guinea-Bissau • Guinea-Bissau

Guinea Ecuatorial
Equatorial Guinea
Kenia • Kenya
Lesoto • Lesotho
Liberia • Liberia
Libia • Libya
Madagascar • Madagascar
Malaui • Malawi
Malí • Mali
Marruecos • Morocco
Mauricio • Mauritius
Mauritania • Mauritania
Mozambique • Mozambique
Namibia • Namibia
Níger • Niger
Nigeria • Nigeria
República Centroafricana
Central African Republic
República Democrática
del Congo • Democratic
Republic of the Congo
Ruanda • Rwanda

Sáhara Occidental
Western Sahara
Santo Tomé y Príncipe
São Tomé and Príncipe
Senegal • Senegal
Sierra Leona • Sierra Leone
Somalia • Somalia
Sudáfrica • South Africa
Sudán • Sudan
Sudán del Sur • South Sudan
Tanzania • Tanzania
Togo • Togo
Túnez • Tunisia
Uganda • Uganda
Zambia • Zambia
Zimbabue • Zimbabwe

Asia • Asia

Bangladesh • Bangladesh

China • China

India • India

Japón • Japan

Jordania • Jordan

Filipinas • Philippines

Corea del Sur • South Korea

Tailandia • Thailand

Turquía • Türkiye (Turkey)

Afganistán • Afghanistan
Arabia Saudita • Saudi Arabia
Armenia • Armenia
Azerbaiyán • Azerbaijan
Bahrein • Bahrain
Bangladesh • Bangladesh
Bhutan • Bhutan
Brunei • Brunei
Camboya • Cambodia
China • China
Corea del Norte • North Korea
Corea del Sur • South Korea
Emiratos Árabes Unidos
United Arab Emirates
Filipinas • Philippines

Georgia • Georgia
India • India
Indonesia • Indonesia
Irán • Iran
Iraq • Iraq
Israel • Israel
Japón • Japan
Jordania • Jordan
Kazajstán • Kazakhstan
Kirguistán • Kyrgyzstan
Kuwait • Kuwait
Laos • Laos
Líbano • Lebanon
Malasia • Malaysia
Maldivas • Maldives

Mongolia • Mongolia
Myanmar (Birmania)
Myanmar (Burma)
Nepal • Nepal
Omán • Oman
Pakistán • Pakistan
Qatar • Qatar
Singapur • Singapore
Siria • Syria
Sri Lanka • Sri Lanka
Tailandia • Thailand
Tayikistán • Tajikistan
Timor Oriental • East Timor
Turkmenistán • Turkmenistan
Turquía • Türkiye (Turkey)

Oceanía • Oceania

Indonesia • Indonesia

Arabia Saudita • Saudi Arabia

Vietnam • Vietnam

Uzbekistán • Uzbekistan
Vietnam • Vietnam
Yemen • Yemen

Australia • Australia

Nueva Zelanda • New Zealand

Australia • Australia
Fiji • Fiji
Islas Salomón • Solomon Islands
Nueva Zelanda • New Zealand
Papua Nueva Guinea • Papua New Guinea
Tasmania • Tasmania
Vanuatu • Vanuatu

partículas y antónimos • particles and antonyms

a, hacia to	**de, desde** from	**para** for	**hacia** toward
encima de over	**debajo de** under	**por** along	**al otro lado** across
delante de in front of	**detrás de** behind	**con** with	**sin** without
sobre onto	**dentro de** into	**antes** before	**después** after
en in	**fuera** out	**antes de** by	**hasta** until
sobre above	**bajo** below	**temprano** early	**tarde** late
dentro inside	**fuera** outside	**ahora** now	**más tarde** later
arriba up	**abajo** down	**siempre** always	**nunca** never
en at	**más allá de** beyond	**con frecuencia** (c **a menudo**) | often	**rara vez** rarely
a través de through	**alrededor de** around	**ayer** yesterday	**mañana** tomorrow
encima de on top of	**al lado de** beside	**primero** m **/ primera** f first	**último** m **/ última** f last
entre between	**en frente de** opposite	**cada** every	**algunos** m **/ algunas** f some
cerca near	**lejos** far	**unos** m **/ unas** f about	**exactamente** exactly
aquí here	**allí** there	**un poco** a little	**mucho** a lot

grande
large

pequeño m / **pequeña** f
small

caliente
hot

frío m / **fría** f
cold

ancho m / **ancha** f
wide

estrecho m / **estrecha** f
narrow

abierto m / **abierta** f
open

cerrado m / **cerrada** f
closed

alto m / **alta** f
tall

corto m / **corta** f
short

lleno m / **llena** f
full

vacío m / **vacía** f
empty

alto m / **alta** f
high

bajo m / **baja** f
low

nuevo m / **nueva** f
new

viejo m / **vieja** f
old

grueso m / **gruesa** f
thick

delgado m / **delgada** f
thin

claro m / **clara** f
(ᶜ **iluminado** m
iluminada f)
light

oscuro m
oscura f
dark

ligero m / **ligera** f
light

pesado m / **pesada** f
heavy

duro m / **dura** f
hard

blando m / **blanda** f
soft

fácil
easy

difícil
difficult

húmedo m / **húmeda** f
wet

seco m / **seca** f
dry

libre
free

ocupado m / **ocupada** f
occupied

bueno m / **buena** f
good

malo m / **mala** f
bad

fuerte
strong

débil
weak

rápido m / **rápida** f
fast

lento m / **lenta** f
slow

gordo m / **gorda** f
fat

delgado m / **delgada** f
thin

correcto m / **correcta** f
correct

incorrecto m / **incorrecta** f
wrong

joven
young

viejo m / **vieja** f
old

limpio m / **limpia** f
clean

sucio m / **sucia** f
dirty

mejor | better

peor | worse

hermoso m / **hermosa** f
(ᶜ **bonito** m / **bonita** f)
beautiful

feo m / **fea** f
ugly

negro m / **negra** f
black

blanco m / **blanca** f
white

interesante
interesting

aburrido m / **aburrida** f
boring

caro m / **cara** f
expensive

barato m / **barata** f
cheap

enfermo m / **enferma** f
sick

bien
well

silencioso m / **silenciosa** f
quiet

ruidoso m / **ruidosa** f
noisy

el principio
beginning

el final
end

frases útiles • useful phrases

frases esenciales
essential phrases

Sí
Yes

No
No

Quizás
Maybe

Por favor
Please

Gracias
Thank you

De nada
You're welcome

Perdone
Excuse me

Lo siento
I'm sorry

No
Don't

Vale
OK

Así vale
That's fine

Está bien
That's correct

Está mal
That's wrong

saludos
greetings

Hola
Hello

Adiós
Goodbye

Buenos días
Good morning

Buenas tardes
Good afternoon

Buenas tardes
Good evening

Buenas noches
Good night

¿Cómo está?
How are you?

Me llamo…
My name is…

¿Cómo se llama?
What is your name?

¿Cómo se llama?
What is his / her name?

Le presento a…
May I introduce…

Este es…
This is…

Encantado de conocerle
Pleased to meet you

Hasta luego
See you later

letreros
signs

Información
Tourist information

Entrada
Entrance

Salida
Exit

Salida de emergencia
Emergency exit

Empuje
Push

Peligro
Danger

Prohibido fumar
No smoking

Fuera de servicio
Out of order

Horario de apertura
Opening times

Entrada libre
Free admission

Rebajado
Reduced

Saldos
Sale

el acceso para silla de ruedas
Wheelchair access

ayuda • help

¿Me puede ayudar?
Can you help me?

No entiendo
I don't understand

No lo sé
I don't know

¿Habla inglés?
Do you speak English?

Hablo inglés
I speak English

Hable más despacio, por favor
Please speak more slowly

¿Me lo puede escribir?
Please write it down for me

Soy sordo *m*
Soy sorda *f*
I'm deaf

Soy ciego *m*
Soy ciega *f*
I'm blind

He perdido…
I have lost…

indicaciones
directions

Me perdí
(C Me he perdido)
I am lost

¿Dónde está el / la…?
Where is the…?

**¿Dónde está el / la…
más cercano / a?**
Where is the nearest…?

**¿Dónde están
los servicios?**
Where is the restroom?

¿Cómo voy a…?
How do I get to…?

A la derecha
To the right

A la izquierda
To the left

Todo recto
Straight ahead

**¿A qué distancia
está…?**
How far is…?

las señales de tránsito (C las señales de tráfico)
road signs

Precaución
Caution

Prohibida la entrada
Do not enter

**Disminuir
velocidad**
Slow down

Desvío | Detour

**Circular por
la derecha**
Keep right

Autopista
Freeway

Prohibido estacionar
(C Prohibido aparcar)
No parking

Callejón sin salida
Dead end

Sentido único
One-way street

Sólo residentes
Residents only

Ceda el paso
Yield

Carretera cortada
Road closed

Obras viales
Roadwork

Curva peligrosa
Dangerous curve

alojamiento
accommodations

Tengo una reservación
(C Tengo una reserva)
I have a reservation

**¿A qué hora es el
desayuno?**
What time is breakfast?

Volveré a las…
I'll be back at… o'clock

**¿Dónde está el
comedor?**
Where is the dining
room?

Me marcho mañana
I'm leaving tomorrow

comida y bebida
eating and
drinking

¡Salud!
Cheers!

**Está
buenísimo / malísimo**
It's delicious / awful

Yo no bebo / fumo
I don't drink / smoke

Yo no como carne
I don't eat meat

Ya no más, gracias
No more for me, thank
you

¿Puedo repetir?
May I have some more?

¿Me trae la cuenta?
May we have the
check?

¿Me da un recibo?
Can I have a receipt?

Zona de fumadores
Smoking area

la salud • health

No me encuentro bien
I don't feel well

Tengo náuseas
I feel sick

Me duele aquí
It hurts here

Tengo fiebre
I have a fever

**Tengo… meses de
embarazo**
I'm… months pregnant

**Necesito una
receta para…**
I need a prescription
for…

**Normalmente
tomo…**
I normally take…

Soy alérgico a…
I'm allergic to…

---

español • english

índice español • Spanish index

español

español

español

español

español

español

español

español

español

español

español

índice inglés · English index

A

abdomen 12
abdominals 16
about 320
above 320
acacia 110
accelerator 200
accessories 36, 38
accident 46
accountant 97, 190
accounting department 175
account number 96
accomodations 323
accused 180
ace 230, 273
Achilles tendon 16
acorn squash 125
acquaintance 24
acquitted 181
across 320
acrylic paint 274
activities 77, 162, 245, 263
actor 191, 254
actors 179
acupressure 55
acupuncture 55
Adam's apple 19
add v 165
addition 58
address 98
adhesive bandage 47
adhesive tape 47
adjustable wrench 80
admissions office 168
admitted 48
adult 23
advantage 230
adventure movie 255
advertisement 269
adzuki beans 131
aerate v 91
Afghanistan 318
Africa 317
after 320
afternoon 305
aftershave 73
aftersun lotion 108
agate 289
agenda 174
aikido 236
air bag 201
air-conditioning 200
aircraft 210
aircraft carrier 215
air filter 202, 204
airliner 210, 212
air mattress 267

airport 212
air tank 239
air vent 210
aisle 106, 168, 210, 254
à la carte 152
alarm clock 70
Albania 316
alcoholic drinks 145
alfalfa 184
Algeria 317
Allen wrench 80
allergy 44
alley 298
alligator 293
alligator clip 167
all meals included 101
all-purpose flour 139
allspice 132
almond 129
almonds 151
almond milk 137
almond oil 134
along 320
alpine 87
alpine skiing 247
alternating current 60
alternator 203
altitude 211
aluminum 289
always 320
Amazon 312
amber ale 145
ambulance 94
amethyst 288
amniocentesis 52
amniotic fluid 52
amount 96
amp 60
amphibians 294
amplifier 268
analog 179
anchor 179, 191, 214, 240
Andes 312
Andorra 316
anesthesiologist 48
angle 164
angler 244
Angola 317
angry 25
animals 290, 292, 294
animated movie 255
ankle 13, 15
ankle-length 34
anniversary 26
annual 86, 307
answer 163
answer v 99, 163
answering machine 99

ant 295
antenna 295
antifreeze 199
Antigua and Barbuda 314
anti-inflammatory 109
antiques store 114
antiseptic 47
antiseptic wipe 47
antiwrinkle 41
antler 291
apartment 59
apartment building 59, 298
apéritif 153
aperture dial 270
apex 164
app 99
app developer 189
appeal 181
appearance 30
appendix 18
appetizer 153
applaud v 255
apple 87
apple corer 68
apple juice 149
appliances 66
application 176
appointment 45, 175
apricot 126
April 306
apron 30, 50, 69, 212
aquamarine 288
Arabian Sea 313
arbor 84
arborio rice 130
arc 164
arch 15, 85, 300
archery 249
architect 190
architecture 300
architrave 301
Arctic Circle 283
Arctic Ocean 312
area 165, 310
areas 299
arena 243
Argentina 315
arithmetic 165
arm 13
armchair 63
Armenia 318
armpit 13
armrest 200, 210
aromatherapy 55
around 320
arrest 94
arrivals 213
arrow 249

art 162
Art Deco 301
artery 19
art history 169
art gallery 261
artichoke 124
artist 274
Art Nouveau 301
arts and crafts 274, 276
art school 169
art supply store 115
arugula 123
ash 283
ashtray 112, 150
Asia 318
asparagus 124
asphalt 187
assault 94
assistant 24
assisted delivery 53
asteroid 280
asthma 44
astigmatism 51
astronaut 281
astronomy 281
asymmetric bars 235
at 320
athlete 234
athletic shoes 31
Atlantic Ocean 312
ATM 97
atmosphere 282, 286
atrium 104
attachment 177
attack 220
attack zone 224
attend v 174
attic 58
attractions 261
auburn 39
audience 254
audioguide 260
August 306
aunt 22
aurora 286
Australia 319
Austria 316
automatic 200
automatic door 196
automatic payment 96
auto racing 249
avalanche 247
avenue 299
avocado 128
awning 148
ax 95
axle 205
ayurveda 55
Azerbaijan 318

B

baby 23, 30
baby formula 52
baby bath 74
baby care 74
baby carriage 75
baby changing room 104
baby monitor 75
baby products 107
baby's breath 110
baby sling 75
back 13, 64
backboard 226
back brush 73
backdrop 254
backgammon 272
backhand 231
backpack 31, 37, 267
backseat 200
backsplash 66
backstroke 239
backswing 233
bacon 118, 157
bacon strip 119
bad 321
badge 94, 189
badminton 231
bag 311
bag cart 233
bagel 139
baggage carousel 212
baggage claim 213
baggage drop 212
baggage trailer 212
bags 37
baguette 138
Bahamas 314
Bahrain 318
bail 181
bailiff 180
bait 244
bait v 245
bake v 67, 138
baked 159
baker 139
bakery 107, 114, 138
baking 69
balance beam 235
balance wheel 276
balcony 59, 254
balcony seats 254
bald 39
bale 184
Balearic Islands 316
ball 15, 75, 221, 224, 226, 228, 230
ball boy 231
ballet 255

english

english

english

english

english

english

english

english

english

english

english

english

english

agradecimientos • acknowledgments

DORLING KINDERSLEY would like to thank senior picture researchers Deepak Negi and Sumedha Chopra, assistant picture researcher Samrajkumar S, and proofreaders Diana Vowles, Heather Wilcox, Catharine Robertson, Chuck Hutchinson, Sam Cooke, Ruth Raisenberger.

The publisher would like to thank the following for their kind permission to reproduce their photographs:
Abbreviations key: (a-above; b-below/bottom; c-centre; f-far; l-left; r-right; t-top)

123RF.com: Aicandy 188fbr; Andriy Popov 34tl; Arthousestudio 265fcla; Astemmer 208c; avigatorphotographer 216bl; Brad Wynnyk 172bc; Cladanifer 25fclb; Daniel Ernst 179tc; Hongqi Zhang 24cla; 175cr; Ingvar Bjork 60c; Koonsiri Scla, 92-93; Kobby Dagan 259c; Kritchanut 25ftl; Lightfieldstudios 35tr; Liubov Vadimovna (Luba) Nel 39cla; Ljupco Smokovski 75crb; Olegtroino 176fcl; Olga Popova 33c; Peopleimages12 41tl; Robert Churchill 94c; Roman Gorielov 33bc; Ruslan Kudrin 35bc, 35br; Subbotina 39cra; Sutichak Yachaingkham 39tc; Tarzhanova 37tc; Vitaly Valua 39tl; Wilawan Khasawong 75cb. **Action Plus:** 224bc; **Alamy Images:** 154t; Alex Segre 150t; A.T. Willett 287bcl; Alex Segre 105ca; Andrew Barker 195fcl; Ambrophoto 24cra; Art Directors & TRIP / Helene Rogers 115bl; artpartner-images.com 181tc; Ben Queenborough 23crb; Boaz Rottem 209cr; Cultura RM 33r; Bernhard Classen 97bc; David Burton 117fbl; Carl DeAbreu 264t; Cavan Images 247fcla; Chicken Strip 112fbr; Chris George 271bc; Destina 176crb; Dorling Kindersley Ltd 266t; Dorling Kindersley Ltd / Vanessa Davies 78fbr; dpa picture alliance 113t; Doug Houghton 107fbr; Doug I loughton 213fclb, Giarini Muratore 195ftr; Henn Martin 182ca; Hideo Kurihara 212t; Hugh Threlfall 35tl; Hugh Threlfall 268bl; Ian Townsley 260cr; Ifeelstock 96cr; Incamerastock / ICP-UK 112fcrb; Issac Rose 54fcr; Jeff Gilbert 213fcrb; keith morris 178c; Majestic Media Ltd / Duncan Thomas 221br, 223crb; Nikreates 268crb; Nathaniel Noir 114bl; MBI 175tl; Michael Foyle 184bl; Olaf Doering 213br; Oleksiy Maksymenko 105tc; Paul Maguire 18t; Pally 294bl; Paul Weston 168br; Prisma Bidagentur AG 246bl; Simone Hogan 241cla; Radharc Images 197cr; Ruslan Kudrin 176tl; Sasa Huzjak 258t; Sergey Kravchenko 37ca; Sergio Azenha 220bc; Stock Connection 287bcr; tarczas 35cr; Ton Koene 213cra; Transport Infrastructures / Paul White 216t; Trekandshoot 194c; Robert Stainforth 98tl; vitaly suprun 176cl; Wavebreak Media Ltd 39cl, 174b, 175tr; Wavebreakmedia Ltd IP-200810 234fcl; **Allsport/Getty Images:** 238cl; **Alvey and Towers:** 241cr; **Anthony Blake Photo Library:** Charlie Stebbings 114cl; **Arcaid:** John Edward Linden 301bl; Martine Hamilton Knight, Architects: Richard Bryant 301br; **Argos:** Vicki Couchman 148cr; **Bosch:** 76tc, 76tcl; **Camera Press:** 38tr, 257cr; Barry J. Holmes 148tr; Jane Hanger 159cr; Mary Germanou 259bc; **Corbis:** 78b; Anna Clopet 247tr; Ariel Skelley / Blend Images 52l; Bettmann 181tr; Bo Zauders 156t; Bob Winsett 247cbl; Brian Bailey 247br; Craig Aurness 215bl; David H.Wells 249cbr; Dennis Marsico 274bl; Dimitri Lundt 236bc; Duomo 211tl; Gail Mooney 277ctcr; George Lepp 248c; Gerald Nowak 239b; Gunter Marx 248cr; Jack Hollingsworth 231bl; James L. Amos 247bl, 191ctr, 220bcr; Jan Butchofsky 277cbc; Johnathan Blair 243cr; Jose F. Poblete 191br; Jose Luis Pelaez.Inc 153tc; Karl Weatherly 220bl, 247tcr; Kelly Mooney Photography 259tl; Kevin Fleming 249bc; Kevin R. Morris 105tr, 243tl, 243tc; Kim Sayer 249ftcr; Lynn Goldsmith 258t; Macduff Everton 231bcl; Mark Gibson 249bl; Mark L. Stephenson 249tcl; Mike King 247cbl; Pablo Corral 115bc; 249ctcl; Paul J. Sutton 224c, 224br; Phil Schermeister 227cb, 248tr; R. W Jones 309; Rick Doyle 241ctr; Robert Holmes 97br, 277ctc; Roger Ressmeyer 169tr; Russ Schleipman 229; The Purcell Team 211ctr; Wally McNamee 220bc, 220bcl, 224bl; Wavebreak Media Ltd 191tc; Yann Arhus-Bertrand 249tl; **Depositphotos Inc:** Londondeposit 262br; **Demetrio Carrasco / Dorling Kindersley (c) Herge / Les Editions Casterman:** 112ccl; **Dixons:** 270t, 270cr, 270bl, 270bcl, 270bcr, 270bc, 270cr; **Dorling Kindersley:** Banbury Museum 35c; Five Napkin Burger 152t; **Dreamstime.com:** Adempercem 197cb; Akesin 191tl; 191cr; Aleksandar Todorovic 300bl; Anan Budtviengpunth 299cra; Andersastphoto 176tc; Andrey Popov 191tb, 55fcra, 190ftr; Anna Eremeeva 82crb; Anna Griessel 25cra; Anna Tolipova 277ftr; Anatoliy Samara 311tc; Anton Matveev 2bl; Arenaphotouk 209tr; Arne9001 190tl; Arne! Manalang 195fbr; Artzzz 203tr; Avagyanlevon 269cla; Birgit Reitz Hofmann 144ca; Bonandbon Dw 154bc; Bright 199tr; Chaos6 26c; Chernetskaya 60tc, 240tc; Christian Offenberg 99ftl; Colicaranica 210t; Dimaberkut 240cr; Dmitry Markov 5fcla, 56-57; Dvmsimages 196bc; Dzmitry Rishchuk 152t; Eakkachai Halang 101ftl; Ekostsov 198fbl; Elena Masiutkina 105fcrb; Ellesi 197br; Evgeny Karandaev 158bc; Exiledphoto 1ca (Golf Balls), 5fcrb, 218tr; Gradts 76ftr; Grigor Ivanov 82bl; Gutaper 176bl; Hasan Can Balcioglu 261c; Hxdbzxy 5cra, 102-103; Hywit Dimyadi 184clb; Iakov Filimonov 115tr; Ivan Danik 4fcrb, 146-147; Ivan Katsarov 201tl; Ilfede 215clb; Imincco 269cc; Isselee 292fcrb; Jamesteoharrt 290br; Jiri Hera 269c; Joe Sohm 259tr; Johncox1958 243ca; Kaspars Grinvalds 172crb; Kenny Tong 5tr, 10-11; Kineticimagery 5bl, 302-303; Konstantinos Moraitis 199tl; Lah 249crb; Larry Gevert 1ca (peppers), 5fcra, 116-117; Leonid Andronov 208clb; Les Daphne 145cb; Leen Beunens 299tl; Lulia Diakova 15tr; Natalia Bratslavsky 101cl; Natvishenka 269tr; Njnightsky 70bl; Nuwan Fernandez 177tr; Maciej Bledowski 95c, 206br; Madrugadaverde 298; Maksim Toome 199ftr; Maniapixel 215tr; Matthias Ziegler 191ftl; Mholod 4fcra, 42-43; Micha Rojek 177tc; Miff32 197bl; Mike_Kiev 199tcr; Mikeal Keal 261cra; Mohamed Osama 75fbl; Monkey Business Images 126b, 100t, 169tl; Monticello 145ftl; Olena Turovtseva 216br; Olga Plugatar 271clb (X2), 271fcla; Pac 268clb; Paolo De Santis 261ftr; Patricia Hofmeester 233cra; Paul Michael Hughes 162tr; Petro Perutskyy 199bl; Phanuwatn 269cl; Photka 213fcra; Ponomarencko 152cr; Roza 300tc; Ryzhov Sergey 138t; Schamie 176cl; Seanlockephotography 189clb; Sean Pavone 301tl; Shariff Che\' Sjors737 277cb; Serghei Starus 190bc; Sergey Galushko 77ftl; Sergey Tolmachyov 270br; Serezniy 48crb; Steafpong 97bl; Sutsaiy 66bl; Takcrane3 198t; Tatiana3337 1ca (multicolor), Theerasak Tammachuen 269cr, 5fclb, 160-161; Trak 256t; Tyler Olson 168crb; Vetkit 189fclb; Volodymyr Melnyk 231ca, 235fcrb; Wang Song 250br, 261cr; Wirestock 169cr; Zerbor 296r; **Education Photos:** John Walmsley 26tl; **Getty Images:** 287tr; 94tr; Corbis Historical / Christopher Pillitz 169cr; George Doyle & Ciaran Griffin 22cr; David Leahy 162tl; DigitalVision / David Leahy 162cla; DigitalVision We Are 227cra; Don Farrall / Digital Vision 176cl; Ethan Miller 270bl; Inti St Clair 179bl; Jeff Bottari 236br; LightRocket / SOPA Images 227ftl; Sean Justice / Digital Vision 24br; The Image Bank / Michael Dunning 235cra; **Getty Images / iStock:** ake1150sb 154bl, AndyOman 304 (Digital Clock X3), Archideaphoto 268t, Babayev 76fcrb, Bluesky85 213tl, Bluestocking 268cb, Bonetta 66fbr, Svetlana Borisov 286cr, Bulgnn 112br, Hadzhi Hristo Chorbadzhi 280tl, DigitalVision Vectors / younglii 96cl, E+ / Adamkaz 206bl, E+ / Aldomurillo 189cra, E+ / AnVr 144bl, E+ / BraunS 231br, E+ / Dean Mitchell 55ftr, E+ / FG Trade 179ftl, E+ / Fly View Productions 96t, E+ / Ivan Pantic 206cb, E+ / Joel Carillet 215br, E+ / JohnnyGreig 104t, E+ / Quavondo 194bw, E+ / Kal9 186bl, 190clb, E+ / Lorado 115bc, E+ / Mbbirdy 66fclb, E+ / Pagadesign 97tr, E+ / Petko Ninov 198fbr, E+ / Satoshi-K 259crb, E+ / SDI Productions 55ftbl, E+ / SolStock 221clb, E+ / South_agency 114br, E+ / Studiocasper 270tc, E+ / Sturti 186bc, E+ / Iashi-Delek 179ftr, E+ / Tempura 48clb, E+ / Tolgart 34br, FamVeld 246tr, Farakos 176cr, FG Trade 188fbl, Gannet77 96c, Grinvalds 99cr, Gumpanat 97cl, Kckate16 188fcla, Kommercialize 208cb, Leedsn 241cra, Sompong Lekhawattana 97tl, LeventKonuk 76cr, Liz Leyden 115tc, LightFieldStudios 169cl, Andrii Lysenko 114tl, Karan Mathur 191cra, MicroStockHub 96clb, Mladn61 196cla, 196-197ca, Moumita Mondal 27fcr, Monkeybusinessimages 49crb, Yaman Mutart 105bl, Nojman 276t, OfirPeretz 195ftl, Prostock-Studio 5clb, 170-171, 188crb, RuslanDashinsky 83tl, Scaliger 208bt, Kazuma Seki 188bl, Deepak Sethi 271ftr, SimonSkafar 1ca (Cornflowers), 188crb, Stockfish Images 215bl, TACrafts 199cra, Teamtime 210b, The Image Bank / Ryan McVay 247cra, Tilo 69ftr, Toxitz 99cl, Alla Tsyganova 148tl, Tunatura 287tc, Universal Images Group / Andia 106t, Andik Tri Witanto 209cra, Chunyip Wong 5crb, 192-193, YakubovAlim 55crb, Zdenkam 23bl, Drazen Zigic 49ftr; **Hulsta:** 70t; **Ideal Standard Ltd:** 72r; **The Image Bank/Getty Images:** 58; **Impact Photos:** Eliza Armstrong 115cr; Philip Achache 246t; **The Interior Archive:** Simon Upton, Architect: Phillippe Starck; **iStockphoto.com:** asterix0597 163tl; EdStock 190br; RichLegg 26bc; **MP Visual.com:** Mark Swallow 202t; **NASA:** 280cr, 280ccl, 281tl; **P & Photos:** 181br; **Plain and Simple Kitchens:** 66t; **Red Consultancy:** Odeon cinemas 257br; **Redferns:** Nigel Crane 259c; **Rex Features:** 106br, 259tc, 259bl, 280b; Charles Ommaney 114tcr; J.F.F Whitehead 243cl; Scott Wiseman 287bl; **Science & Society Picture Library:** Science Museum 202b; **Science Photo Library:** IBM Research 190cla; NASA 281cr; **Shutterstock.com:** Africa Studio 198bl, Akkalak Aiempradit 260cla, BearFotos 245clb, Rauda Bercan 213fbl, Comebuad Images 24bl, Odin Daniel 214bl, Diamant24 60fclb, Early Spring 100br, Dmytro Falkowskyi 196-197cb, Giuseppe_R 4fbr, 252-253, Kaspars Grinvalds 1ca (Shirts), 5ftr, 28-29, 175clb, Ground Picture 26ftr, 100fbr, Haveseen 264b, HelloRF Zcool 168t, Joseph Hendrickson 59tl, Nigel Jarvis 214bc, Mkfilm 287br, New Africa 71tr, 75br, 77cra, Eline Oostingh 215cb, SeventyFour 232bl, Ilya Sviridenko 185fbr, Alla Tsyganova 114fbl, zcw 77ca; **SuperStock:** Ingram Publishing 62; Juanma Aparicio / age fotostock 172t; **Sony:** 268bc; **Neil Sutherland:** 82tr, 90t, 118, 188cr, 196tr, 299cl, 299bl; **Vauxhall:** 199cl, 200, **Colin Walton:** 99tcl, 401.

DK PICTURE LIBRARY:
Akhil Bahkshi; Patrick Baldwin; Geoff Brightling; British Museum; John Bulmer; Andrew Butler; Joe Cornish; Brian Cosgrove; Andy Crawford and Kit Hougton; Philip Dowell; Alistair Duncan; Gables; Bob Gathany; Norman Hollands; Kew Gardens; Peter James Kindersley; Vladimir Kozlik; Sam Lloyd; London Northern Bus Company Ltd; Tracy Morgan; David Murray and Jules Selmes; Musée Vivant du Cheval, France; Museum of Broadcast Communications; Museum of Natural History; NASA; National History Museum; Norfolk Rural Life Museum; Stephen Oliver; RNLI; Royal Ballet School; Guy Ryecart; Science Museum; Neil Setchfield; Ross Simms and the Winchcombe Folk Police Museum; Singapore Symphony Orchestra; Smart Museum of Art; Tony Souter; Erik Svensson and Jeppe Wikstrom; Sam Tree of Keygrove Marketing Ltd; Barrie Watts; Alan Williams; Jerry Young.

Additional photography by Colin Walton.

Colin Walton would like to thank:
A&A News, Uckfield; Abbey Music, Tunbridge Wells; Arena Mens Clothing, Tunbridge Wells; Burrells of Tunbridge Wells; Gary at Di Marco's; Jeremy's Home Store, Tunbridge Wells; Noakes of Tunbridge Wells; Ottakar's, Tunbridge Wells; Selby's of Uckfield; Sevenoaks Sound and Vision; Westfield, Royal Victoria Place, Tunbridge Wells.

All other images © Dorling Kindersley

español • english